IN THIS HOUR

"Hesed v'emet al-ya'azvucha—Let not kindness and truth forsake you" (Proverbs 3:3)

In gratitude to Dr. D. Walter Cohen *z"l* for his devotion to knowledge and for his exemplary leadership of and support for the Jewish Publication Society

—FROM THE JPS BOARD OF TRUSTEES

UNIVERSITY OF NEBRASKA PRESS   LINCOLN

IN THIS HOUR

HESCHEL'S WRITINGS IN NAZI GERMANY AND LONDON EXILE

Abraham Joshua Heschel

FOREWORD BY *Susannah Heschel*
EDITED AND ANNOTATED BY *Helen Plotkin*
TRANSLATIONS BY *Stephen Lehmann* AND *Marion Faber*

THE JEWISH PUBLICATION SOCIETY   PHILADELPHIA

All rights reserved. Published by the University of
Nebraska Press as a Jewish Publication Society book.
Manufactured in the United States of America.

Names: Heschel, Abraham Joshua, 1907–1972,
author. | Heschel, Susannah, author of foreword.
| Plotkin, Helen C., editor. | Lehmann, Stephen,
translator. | Faber, Marion, translator.
Title: In this hour: Heschel's writings in Nazi
Germany and London exile / Abraham Joshua
Heschel; foreword by Susannah Heschel; edited
and annotated by Helen Plotkin; translations
by Stephen Lehmann and Marion Faber.
Description: Lincoln: University of Nebraska
Press, [2019] | "Published by the University of
Nebraska Press as a Jewish Publication Society
book." | Includes bibliographical references.
Identifiers: LCCN 2018047755
ISBN 9780827613225 (cloth: alk. paper)
ISBN 9780827617988 (epub)
ISBN 9780827617995 (mobi)
ISBN 9780827618251 (pdf)
Subjects: LCSH: Judaism—20th century. | Jewish
philosophy—20th century. | Tannaim—Biography.
| Abravanel, Isaac, 1437–1508. | Jewish education.
Classification: LCC BM580 .H47 2019 |
DDC 296—dc23 LC record available at
https://lccn.loc.gov/2018047755.

Set in Questa by Mikala R. Kolander.
Designed by N. Putens.

In this hour we, the living, are "the people of Israel." The tasks, begun by our patriarchs and prophets and continued by their descendants, are now entrusted to us. We are either the last Jews or those who will hand over the entire past to generations to come. We will either forfeit or enrich the legacy of the ages.

ABRAHAM JOSHUA HESCHEL, *The Earth Is the Lord's*

CONTENTS

FOREWORD

Susannah Heschel

When my father arrived in Berlin as a twenty-year-old student in 1927, he thought he had arrived at the center of the intellectual universe. He was dazzled by the scholarly riches not only at the University of Berlin, but also at the two rabbinical seminaries, Orthodox and Liberal, all located at the heart of the city, a neighborhood that also was home to thousands of Polish Jews, recent immigrants. An abundance of synagogues led by learned rabbis appealed to him, though he most often attended the small Orthodox synagogue of Rabbi Yehiel Weinberg, one of the deeply learned authorities on *halachah* (Jewish law) and also a person of great charm and warmth; when I was a child, we visited him in Montreux, Switzerland.

Berlin in the late 1920s was a city of great theater, concerts, lectures, and intense conversations and debates. As a child, I loved asking my father about his student days and imagining what his life was like. He was terribly poor; often he could afford to eat only potatoes for weeks on end. He would rent a room from a Jewish family, either near the university or in Charlottenburg, a neighborhood with mostly middle-class German Jews. Often other students also rented rooms with those families, and my father enjoyed the intellectual exchanges with them. He described his student years as filled with intense study—indeed, he was always reading, either a Hasidic text or a work of philosophy—but he also enjoyed the excitement of Weimar culture. Always wanting to explore and understand different ways of thinking, he took courses at both the Orthodox and Liberal

Jewish seminaries, and was one of very few students to have been welcome at both. Although he already had received Orthodox rabbinical ordination while in Warsaw from Rabbi Menachem Ziemba, he wanted to know how liberal Jews approached classical Jewish texts. The weekly "salon" he joined at the home of Jewish sociologist David Koigen on Mommsenstrasse was a chance for intense discussion of the Jewish future. On other evenings my father would go to poetry recitations, often of the poet Stefan George, though he was more inclined to the work of Rilke.

My father was part of a generation of Jewish thinkers who were both products of the great German intellectual and scholarly achievements and, at the same time, severe critics of German ways of thinking. Philology had certainly accomplished much in the study of religious texts, but it was not able to convey the essential significance of those texts: why people are religious. There was something deadening, he thought, about the synagogue services in Germany: a formality and regulation of behavior that my father felt hindered rather than enhanced prayer. The intensity of religious devotion he had experienced in the Hasidic world of Warsaw was for him authentic Jewish piety.

Just a month after my father completed his doctoral dissertation, *Das prophetische Bewusstsein*, a study of prophetic consciousness, in December 1932, everything changed. With Hitler in power, it became impossible for my father to find a publisher for his dissertation, and without publication, he could not receive the PhD degree he needed to obtain a teaching position at a university. He continued teaching, writing, and lecturing to the Jewish community, and in 1935 he published a biography of Maimonides that was received with great praise. Shortly after, he published a small book on Abravanel, as well as several articles on medieval Jewish philosophy. Soon his dissertation appeared, published by the Polish Academy of Arts and Sciences. The reviewers were full of praise, and his work came to be widely known in Europe and also in the United States.

But how to escape the Third Reich? My father was offered a

position at the rabbinical college in Prague that was supposed to open, but could not. Martin Buber invited him to direct the Jüdisches Lehrhaus, an institute for adult Jewish learning that Buber and Franz Rosenzweig had founded, and my father moved in 1936 from Berlin to Frankfurt. While there, he helped Buber learn to speak modern Hebrew in the months before Buber left for Palestine.

Throughout those years, my father remained a deeply pious Jew in every respect, and he stayed close to his family—his mother and his sisters Gittel and Esther in Warsaw and his other siblings in Vienna: his brother, Jacob, his sister Devorah and her husband, Aryeh Leib Dermer, and his eldest sister, Sarah, who was married to the Kopycznitzer Rebbe. My father rented a room with an Orthodox Jewish family in Frankfurt, in the center of the city on Hansaallee; later he rented a room in the large home of another Jewish family, on a quiet street in the suburb of Eschersheim. It was in that leafy neighborhood he was arrested late one night in October 1938, held in terrible conditions at a police station, then put on a train and deported to the Polish border. He spent the next ten months in Warsaw trying to obtain the visa to the United States that Dr. Julian Morgenstern, president of the Hebrew Union College in Cincinnati, Ohio, had procured for him. Ultimately my father arrived in the United States "as a brand plucked from the fires" in March 1940, after a brief few months living with his brother, who had escaped with his family to London.

My father would never return to Germany, nor to Poland, and he suffered terribly when he spoke of the fate of his family and friends. Yet he retained the positive memories of his student years and enjoyed describing those experiences. Certainly he was shaped intellectually by what he learned, though much of his scholarship was written as a critique of the limitations of the German world of scholarship. Nonetheless, he lived in the world of scholarship, and he often talked about the expectation of his youth that he would become a professor at a German university. Who could imagine what would happen, he used to say to me when we took our walks together.

Even as he was immersed in his scholarship, my father was always concerned with his fellow Jews and the state of their spirit. He wrote to offer not comfort but challenge, yet in his words of challenge from the 1930s there is always hope: "moral and spiritual recovery in the face of political catastrophe." He spoke of German Jews as inverted Marranos who had become Jewish on the outside and Christian on the inside, lacking a sense of what it means to be imbued with a Jewish spirit. In one of his first visits for tea at Buber's home in Heppenheim in 1936, my father challenged Buber's assertion that adult Jews need to learn the words of the prayers: what we need to teach is not the prayer book, but how to pray, my father said.

The essays that Stephen Lehmann discovered in German Jewish publications and among my father's papers now appear in this volume for the first time, in a felicitous translation that he and Marion Faber prepared. They give us a remarkable picture of how my father, at such a young age—still in his twenties—sought to give insight and also comfort to the Jews of Germany prior to his own deportation to Poland in October 1938. Many of the themes we hear are echoed in my father's later writings, after he became a professor in the United States. Special thanks go to Helen Plotkin, who prepared excellent notes for the volume that clarify points of reference and also edited my father's notes for his lecture in London.

This volume opens a new view of the experience of German Jews in their years between dignity and despair and demonstrates the remarkable vitality of the young Abraham Joshua Heschel, one of the extraordinary figures of Jewish history.

ACKNOWLEDGMENTS

For invaluable help of all kinds we thank Edward K. Kaplan, Larry Hankin (*Intermountain Jewish News*), Sven-Erik Rose, Richard Schuldenfrei, Barry Schwartz (The Jewish Publication Society), Patrick A. Stawski (Duke University Libraries), Regina Stein, and Joy Weinberg (The Jewish Publication Society). We are grateful that the Jewish Publication Society and the University of Nebraska Press share our conviction that these writings deserve publication in English. A special debt of gratitude goes to Susannah Heschel, whose warm encouragement and support made this project possible.

Fig. 1. The front page of the *Gemeindeblatt der jüdischen Gemeinde zu Berlin*, May 17, 1936

INTRODUCTION

This book offers translations of selected writings by Abraham Joshua Heschel from his years in Nazi-ruled Germany and his months in London before he made his way to the United States, where he ceased writing in German. Many of the pieces were written for the official news organ of Berlin's Jewish community, and most have not been translated until now.

As a collection, it is *about* Jewish teaching and learning, and at the same time it is a book *of* Jewish teaching and learning. It is a plea for spiritually rich Jewish education as well as a demonstration of what that education requires.

The curriculum embodied here is many layered. Even as he teaches history, Heschel teaches more than history: the old becomes new, and the struggles of one era shed light on another. The famously inaccessible Talmud and the concerns of a medieval scholar take on compelling immediacy. Even as Heschel quotes ancient sources, his words address the issues of his own time and speak urgently to ours.

The collection consists of five parts:

1. The text of a speech Heschel gave in London in 1940 in which he laid out with passion his vision for Jewish education, along with the notes he embedded within that speech critiquing the forms of Jewish education in the modern era
2. Eight essays, written in 1936, on the Rabbis of the mishnaic period

3. A biographical study of Don Yitzhak Abravanel, written in 1937
4. Three articles written for Jewish holidays in Berlin in 1936 and 1937
5. A set of four meditations, recently discovered among Heschel's papers, that address the issues he grappled with as he experienced the horrors unfolding around him

Composed during a time of intense crisis for European Jewry, these writings argue for and exemplify a powerful vision of Jewish learning and its redemptive role in the past and the future of the Jewish people.

Heschel's Education

Born in Warsaw in 1907, Abraham Joshua Heschel was descended on both sides of his family from eminent Hasidic rabbis, and he grew up in a deeply religious environment. His path of study began in his earliest childhood. He received the best religious education the Hasidic world had to offer, and he wore his aristocratic heritage well, excelling in both the intellectual and spiritual realms. At age sixteen he received rabbinical ordination, having become expert in the entire corpus of Jewish lore, including Bible, Talmud, legal codes, mystical works, and the commentaries of the Hasidic masters.

His introduction to modernity came while he was still in Warsaw, where he began reading secular Jewish writings in Yiddish and modern Hebrew, making mentors of their authors. His first published poem, *"Se Zilbert zin azoy loyter . . ."* (The womanly skin silvers so purely . . .), appeared in 1926 in the Yiddish anthology *Varshaver Shriftn*. And with this step, according to Heschel's biographers, Edward Kaplan and Samuel Dresner, "Heschel took his place among Sholem Asch, Yitzhak Bashevis (pen name of I. B. Singer), Max Weinrich," and other eminent Yiddish poets.[1] The world of learning and culture beyond the traditional Jewish curriculum had opened up for him, and he set his sights on a university education.

To meet the university entrance requirements, he moved to Vilna and enrolled at the Real-Gymnasium, a secondary school operated by Jews. The topics of study were the sciences, mathematics, languages, and literature. His teachers were intellectuals of the highest order; the pedagogy was progressive and rigorous. All classes were taught in Yiddish.

While he remained scrupulously observant of Jewish law and spiritually engaged with the Jewish God, Heschel was already a worldly and educated man by the time he graduated from the Gymnasium and left Warsaw for Berlin at age twenty.

As Susannah Heschel writes in her vivid foreword, her father, raised in the intense piety of Hasidism, responded affirmatively to German learning (much less so to German Jewish religious practice). But the experience of secular education at its best also revealed to Heschel its profound deficiencies. In an autobiographical piece composed in 1953 he wrote:

> I came with great hunger to the University of Berlin to study philosophy. I looked for a system of thought, for the depth of the spirit, for the meaning of existence. Erudite and profound scholars gave courses in logic, epistemology, esthetics, ethics and metaphysics. They opened the gates of the history of philosophy. I was exposed to the austere discipline of unremitting inquiry and self-criticism. I communed with the thinkers of the past who knew how to meet intellectual adversity with fortitude, and learned to dedicate myself to the examination of basic premises at the risk of failure.
>
> Yet, in spite of the intellectual power and honesty which I was privileged to witness, I became increasingly aware of the gulf that separated my views from those held at the university. I had come with a sense of anxiety: how can I rationally find a way where ultimate meaning lies, a way of living where one would never miss a reference to supreme significance? Why am I here at all, and what is my purpose? I did not even know how to phrase my concern. But to my teachers that was a question unworthy of philosophical analysis. . . .
>
> The problem to my professors was how to be good. In my ears the question rang: how to be holy.[2]

In 1927 Heschel enrolled at the University of Berlin, majoring in philosophy and minoring in art history and Semitic philology. At the same time, he enrolled at the Hochschule für die Wissenschaft des Judentums (Academy for the Science of Judaism), a rabbinical seminary, and he taught Talmud there as well. While his graduation from the Hochschule included a second ordination, what Heschel sought there was education, not ordination. Following the program of the *Wissenschaft* movement, which aimed to ground Jewish learning in the tradition of German scholarship, the school utilized the most rigorous and objective scholarly methods to study Jewish history, texts, and theology. There Heschel was introduced to "higher criticism," including "source criticism," using historical research methodology to investigate the Bible as a product of human hands—the accumulation of multiple voices and layers of historical development—as opposed to the singular revealed word of God. As a "liberal" institution, the Hochschule walked a fine line: Heschel's teachers there distanced themselves on the one hand from the most radical reformers, who saw traditional Jewish practice as outmoded, and, on the other, from proponents of the Orthodox movement—which had arisen to counter Reform—who viewed academic investigation and historical analysis of traditional texts as sacrilege unless it was formulated explicitly to defend those texts.

In 1930 Heschel began to work on his dissertation in philosophy at the university. Writing about prophetic consciousness in the Hebrew Bible, he used his newly acquired philosophical language to approach his own beloved texts in a new way. His dissertation was approved in 1933, but before his degree would be granted he was required to find a publisher willing to publish the dissertation as a book.

This task took nearly three years, and the tale of its accomplishment is gripping. Compounding the enormous stumbling blocks created by the politically and financially troubled times, Heschel had difficulty finding a home for his work because it straddled genres. It used the language of philosophy and psychology to discuss a passionate God in anthropomorphic terms. When it was published in English in 1963 as *The Prophets*, it became, and remains today, one of Heschel's most beloved works. It is careful, rigorous, and informative, yet it opens the heart and tugs at the spirit of the reader.

Living and Writing in Berlin

Heschel's first book was a biography of Maimonides, commissioned in 1934 by the Jewish publisher Erich Reiss, for whom Heschel was working as an editor in Berlin. (Reiss's confidence in Heschel would finally make the difference in bringing his dissertation to publication.) The biography, which Heschel completed on very short notice, was a commemoration of Maimonides's 800th birthday in the following year. It was widely praised, both for making scholarship accessible and for its literary qualities. The following year it was translated into French, and finally, in 1982, into English.

In 1937, for the 500th birthday of the Spanish-born Jewish statesman, financier, and theologian Yitzhak Abravanel, Erich Reiss commissioned a second commemorative biography, offered in its entirety in English for the first time in this volume. Meanwhile, Heschel was producing a steady stream of articles for Jewish journals and newspapers. From 1936 to 1938 he wrote for the *Gemeindeblatt der jüdischen Gemeinde zu Berlin* (the official newspaper of the Jewish community of Berlin). Founded in 1911 and shut down in 1938, the *Gemeindeblatt* was, at the time Heschel wrote for it, a weekly newspaper with a circulation exceeding fifty thousand, making it the most widely received Jewish publication in the country. Heschel's pieces for the newspaper ranged from very short book notices, reviews, and news items to page-long articles instructing readers in their preparations for Jewish holidays. The series entitled "Personalities in Jewish History," included in this volume, was his most sustained effort for the *Gemeindeblatt*.

Heschel wrote the pieces collected here during a period of unspeakable difficulties for Germany's Jews, though much worse was to come. The Berlin Olympics, held in the summer of 1936, provided a brief respite from the most flagrant signs of persecution—coincidentally, the games closed on the same day that the last installment of Heschel's Personalities series was published—but the German government's harassment of its country's Jews was relentless. "The utter bleakness of our situation. . . . We are completely isolated," writes the diarist Victor Klemperer on April 28 of that year.[3] The Nuremberg Laws, enacted the previous year, codified the Jews' exclusion from German civic life, and readers of the *Gemeindeblatt* were turning to the paper for help with finding employment, negotiating the complications of their new legal status, and preparing for emigration.

The *Gemeindeblatt* was only one of numerous institutional resources German Jewry turned to for direction and sustenance between the Nazi takeover in 1933 and the pogrom known as Kristallnacht on November 9, 1938, which conclusively shattered any remaining illusions of Jewish security and autonomy. In the short time left to it, Jewish existence in Germany was to become increasingly segregated, increasingly precarious. Under the watchful eye of Nazi authorities, the Jewish Cultural Alliance (Jüdischer Kulturbund) managed to run a lively cultural program throughout Germany for Jewish audiences, giving work to otherwise unemployable Jewish actors and musicians. Jewish publishing houses and journals gained new importance as forums for Jewish thought.

The Centrality of Adult Education

That German Jewry was in the throes of an unprecedented and existential crisis was clear to everyone. But to religious Jews like Heschel, the political crisis laid bare a long-simmering spiritual crisis. Even as Judaic studies in Germany reached a pinnacle of excellence, the great Jewish thinkers had, over the previous decades, become aware that German Jewish life was growing increasingly impoverished. The emphasis on the scientific that characterized the work of the great scholars at institutions such as the Hochschule and the rapid cultural assimilation that was the rule among German Jews had left much of the community bereft of a spiritual center, with little connection to God and tradition.

It was against this background that, in 1920, the philosopher of Judaism Franz Rosenzweig had opened the Frankfurt Freies Jüdisches Lehrhaus (Free Jewish House of Learning), a pioneering effort in adult education aimed at facilitating a return to an authentic spiritual life through the study of Jewish texts. Growing up in an assimilated family, Rosenzweig became a well-educated European, but had little exposure to Jewish content. When his own life was changed by the discovery of Jewish learning, he sought to make it available to others from his own cultural milieu. At the height of its popularity, more than one thousand adult Jews participated in the programs of the Frankfurt Lehrhaus. Historian Martin Jay describes it like this: "Rather than serving as an outreach program of the scholarly and 'objective' *Wissenschaft des Judentums* or a seminary for the propagation of the Halakhah (law), it sought to foster what Rosenzweig in his inaugural address of October 11, 1920, 'On Jewish Learning,' called a restoration of Judaism as a whole way of life."[4]

Rosenzweig's pedagogy was innovative—collaborative learning rather than the usual lecture format. Yet it never really took off, and due to his illness and early death from amyotrophic lateral sclerosis, his Lehrhaus closed in 1929. Nonetheless, his vision of a Judaism rediscovered and revitalized by drawing a broad range of adult Jews into spiritually rich learning was an inspiration for Jews throughout Germany. Even the Berlin adult school, though founded a year before the Frankfurt Lehrhaus, came to be known as a Lehrhaus, in manifest homage to the Frankfurt model.

In 1933, the Frankfurt Lehrhaus reopened under the leadership of Martin Buber (1879–1965), and in 1935 Buber invited Heschel to teach a course there.

At the time, Buber was among a number of prominent Jews in Germany who had developed a deep interest in the traditions of their Eastern European brothers and sisters, the Jews of Poland, Russia, and Lithuania. They saw the Eastern European Jews, sometimes nostalgically, as representing a lost world of piety and connectedness. Buber had experienced that world for a time in his childhood but had distanced himself from his Orthodox upbringing. When he discovered the spiritual richness of Eastern European Hasidism as an adult, he proceeded to make the collection and preservation of Hasidic tales one of his central endeavors.

Buber and Heschel had taken opposite journeys across the territory between Eastern European Hasidism and Western European scientific intellectualism, and their paths crossed at their mutual commitment to finding a synthesis. Heschel, the Polish Jew rooted in Hasidism, studying, teaching, and writing in Berlin and Frankfurt, embodied within himself that synthesis—something Buber surely must have admired.

Though its educational impact may have been disappointing, the Lehrhaus was an important symbol of how traditional and modern sensibilities might come together to create truly transformative adult education. Shortly after Heschel's Personalities series was published in the *Gemeindeblatt*, Buber recruited Heschel to move to Frankfurt to teach and help administer Lehrhaus programs, and just as Heschel was undertaking the move, the December 1936 issue of the influential German Jewish periodical *Der Morgen* published an article on Buber's Lehrhaus. The article, by Eduard Strauss, a close associate of Buber's and an acquaintance of Heschel's, gives us a sense of the role the Lehrhaus played in German Jewish consciousness and makes explicit the connection between the Frankfurt Lehrhaus and the Rabbis about whom Heschel had written in the *Gemeindeblatt* a few months before:

> Since the first Beit Midrash in Yavne became a reality in our history, the Lehrhaus derives its legitimization from the Jewish fate. It emerged and continually emerges in answer to the call that emanates from the Now. For the Jew's response to the plight in which the call of God finds him is always: to learn. We always remember and recount, for ourselves and for those who will come after us: learning and teaching is what fills our awareness with what is present and, passing through us, links the past with the

future. In our learning and teaching the spirit renews the covenant in all times: in the Lehrhaus all Jewish reality stretches out to the present generation hands from the past to support it and hands from the future to guide it.[5]

Throughout his *Gemeindeblatt* pieces, Heschel renders the talmudic term *beit midrash* into German as Lehrhaus (we use "House of Learning" in our translation), which his readers would surely have understood in the context Strauss describes. The ancient House of Learning would be modeled in their imaginations on the Lehrhaus of Rosenzweig and Buber.

Heschel was deported from Germany to Poland just before Kristallnacht, and then escaped from Poland to England barely two months before the German invasion. Half a year after arriving in London, he founded the Institute for Jewish Learning (IJL)—the London Lehrhaus. The fact that he opened the IJL in London practically the minute he set foot on solid land, even though he was not planning to make the city his permanent home, shows how central this focus on Jewish learning was to his thinking and his goals. The speech he gave at its founding, included as the first piece in this volume, is a profound expression of his hopes for learning as a source of "moral and spiritual recovery in the face of political catastrophe"—a phrase he uses to describe the innovations of Rabbi Johanan ben Zakkai. If the German Lehrhaus represented the new Yavne—a place for Jewish renewal in exile—then perhaps the London incarnation represented the Yavne that must always travel with the Jews, reinventing itself wherever they would land, finding stability in the very act of constant renewal.

About This Volume

The core of this volume is a collection of works written by Abraham Joshua Heschel in 1936 and 1937 while he was living in Berlin, then the capital of Nazi Germany. The pieces in parts 2 and 4, "Personalities in Jewish History" and "For the Jewish Holidays in Berlin," were originally published in the *Gemeindeblatt*. Part 3, on the life and thought of the late medieval rabbi and statesman Don Yitzhak Abravanel, was published as a monograph in Germany in 1937 and in Polish translation the following year.

All these writings were educational offerings to the German Jewish community in the throes of catastrophe. At first some of their content might seem a strange choice: most of them are framed as histories of times long gone; some of them largely comprise arrangements of quotations from the Talmud; and they do not preach directly of courage or comfort. But as we worked on translating and annotating these pieces, we became increasingly aware of their remarkable, innovative qualities, and we heard with increasingly clarity an underlying theme: they simultaneously argue for and exemplify a powerful vision of Jewish learning—emphasizing its redemptive role in the past and the future of the Jewish people.

It was therefore with great excitement that we discovered, in the Heschel archives at Duke University, the draft of a speech Heschel had delivered on January 30, 1940, at the opening of his Institute for Jewish Learning in London. He did not prepare the lecture for publication, and it is not known how closely "The Idea of Jewish Education" matches what he actually said that day. Nevertheless, we have presented it as an introduction to the other works in the volume, in the first part, "London: Jewish Learning in Exile," because it articulates with passion his critique not only of Jewish educational strategies, but also of Jewish spiritual life in the early twentieth century. Indeed, his prescriptions for integrated Jewish learning remain significant and relevant in the early twenty-first century.

Embedded within Heschel's typescript are notes for a "speech within a speech" on the history of Jewish education in the modern era. Our text presents the body of the speech in the form of an essay, followed by the lecture notes Heschel included midway. In extensive endnotes we have provided explanatory information to help fill in some of the gaps.

Part 2 contains the series of essays entitled "Personalities in Jewish History" published in the *Gemeindeblatt* between February and August

1936: eight biographical sketches of Rabbinic figures, set in the century and a half following the destruction of the Second Temple in 70 CE. Through the lens of these eight lives Heschel portrays the Jewish community's response to terrible oppression by Roman imperialists and chronicles the reunification and rebuilding of a new Jewish society by means of a renewed emphasis on both learning and tradition. We have prefaced this part with a historical review and explanation of terms.

Heschel's main source materials for these essays are short vignettes from ancient Jewish literature, primarily the Talmud. In their original context, these vignettes are not presented as history or biography—they are brief bits of lore brought up for various reasons in the midst of legal discussions and biblical interpretation. Relying on his vast knowledge of these sources (he had a prodigious memory), Heschel collected, sorted, and reassembled them, filling in the gaps when called for. He presents the Rabbis as complex leaders and scholars who responded to the events of their times and whose strengths, weaknesses, and personal styles shaped the future of Judaism.

In reformulating the tales of the Rabbis as history, Heschel responded to the educational revolution that defined the modern era and informed his own educational experience. The centrality of history—of historical research as the primary and most legitimate lens for approaching religion—was a major innovation of modernity. Rendering stories that were once accessible only in a religious context into the genre of historical narrative made them available for the first time to many in his audience of modern German Jews.

What is truly unique about Heschel's presentation is that it is never *merely* history. His discussion of Rabbi Johanan ben Zakkai, the first sage to take up the challenge of defining a new form of Judaism that would function without the Temple, demonstrates Heschel's nuanced sense of the role of historical change in the Jewish story: "For the people, the sanctuary in Jerusalem was the visual manifestation of the Beyond, an enduring miracle. . . . To what concrete symbol should the energy that stemmed from devotion and wonder now turn? Through

Rabbi Johanan ben Zakkai the *myth of learnedness* came into being."
To describe Rabbi Johanan ben Zakkai's new subject for devotion
and wonder—learning—as a myth with a definable starting point,
as a deliberate construction rather than an eternal reality, is to take
up the methods of historical criticism. But Heschel does not imply
that this perspective lessens the spiritual power or significance of
the new construct. He does not suggest that the sage's move was
cynically pragmatic. For Heschel, an embrace of historical thinking
was not an inevitable move toward secularism, but rather a way to
enhance the connection to authentic Jewish life.

Mirroring the relationship between his Hasidic roots and his *Wissenschaft* learning, Heschel uses ancient materials to construct a
modern story that never loses touch with the spiritual texture of the
original. He transforms a set of vignettes from disparate sources,
written down as part of a very different project, into a narrative
that speaks directly to the contemporary situation of his readers.
In presenting the ways in which the leadership of a besieged and
imperiled Jewish community responded to oppression and dispersal, the parallels to the situation of German Jews didn't have
to be—indeed, couldn't be—spelled out. By describing a century
and a half of remarkable innovation and invention in the service of
reclaiming tradition, these biographies suggest that the lives and
accomplishments of the early Rabbis exemplify the possibilities not
just of Jewish renewal but of an unbroken, ongoing continuity. For
his readers at the time, these essays offered what has come to be
known as spiritual resistance.

The biographical study of Don Yitzhak Abravanel (1437–1509)
in part 3 of this volume is also deeply concerned with history. For
Heschel, the story of Abravanel is, in part, a vehicle for teaching his
audience the story of the expulsion of the Jews, first from Spain and
then from Portugal in the late fifteenth century. Heschel prefaced
this biography with an italicized meditation on history as the medium
in which the human encounter with God plays out. Through the
lens of Abravanel's life, Heschel explores the implications of Jewish

participation in the political and financial leadership of the non-Jewish world at a time of persecution and dispersal. And through Abravanel's writings, Heschel explores a philosophy that reclaims relationship with God in response to the frenzy of pure rationalism.

In contemplating both Abravanel's life and works, Heschel presents history as a theme, for good and for bad: Historical thinking was the innovative genius of Abravanel's biblical interpretation (in fact, Heschel calls Abravanel "the true founder of *Wissenschaft des Judentums*") as well as the driving force behind Abravanel's commitment to tradition. But it was also the source of Abravanel's tragic error—messianism. He stood proudly on the historical stage, "collaborating with the drama of the political, social and economic powers," but ultimately, he was "pulverized . . . by the winds," "a symbol of the last act of Jewish history in Europe." Heschel ends on a note of chilly comfort, suggesting that the forced exit of the Jews from the halls of power in Spain saved them from becoming collaborators in the bloody conquest of the New World.

Part 4 contains three essays. The first two, related to the High Holidays, focus on the themes of *teshuvah*: repentance, renewal, and return. In "The Power of Repentance," Heschel lets the tradition speak for itself: the essay consists entirely of quotations from the Talmud and other Rabbinic texts, uncluttered by explanation or interpretation. Yet simply by gathering these lines from their disparate sources and assembling them as a tapestry, he has created something new: an expansive and multifaceted expression of how repentance might be understood. The second essay, "The Meaning of Repentance," was published three days after "The Power of Repentance."[6] These essays, written for Rosh Hashanah, 1936, are really two parts of one whole.

The third piece on the Jewish holidays in Berlin, "Lights over the Sea," is a work of fiction—a rare medium for Heschel. It was published in November 1937, eleven months before the Gestapo arrested and deported him to his native Poland, and not quite two years before he left his homeland forever, fleeing first to England and finally to

America. This story depicts contemporary Jews on the cusp of change and spotlights Heschel's cautious hope for their future.

The story might best be characterized as a parable. Like the parables of ancient midrash, it is carefully constructed, each element hiding layered meaning. In the opening scene, the ship's passengers are complacent. The sun is about to set, and they have every reason to expect darkness to fall—both because of the signs in the sky and because it has happened so many times before—but, blinded by their complacency, they are surprised nevertheless. Once darkness sets in, the three Jewish passengers are moved to a new awareness: it's Hanukkah. The eldest of the three is the only one who knows the ritual and its meaning, but it falls to the youngest to invent a clever way to make the ritual work in their new environment: rigging up a stand for the menorah in transit, balancing it on a suitcase in front of a porthole. As the three Jews handle the precious family heirloom they are carrying across the sea, the youngest bemoans his lack of Jewish knowledge and declares his desire to learn. The memories of the eldest come to life. The world they have known disappears behind them, and they are overtaken by an impulse to reclaim their Jewish heritage. Heschel perceived his own community to be in urgent need of such reclamation.

Before the Holocaust, there were two candidates for the most devastating blow to Jewish civilization: the destruction of the Second Temple and the expulsion from Spain. Now, as Heschel stands at the beginning of the European horror, he expresses his confidence that the refugees' true refuge will be the reclamation of tradition through learning. The characters in his story are on their way from a shaky Jewish past to an unimaginable Jewish future. They need a way to bring their identity with them, even though it is in tatters and does not seem to fit their new environment.

This collection closes in part 5 with four short meditations. The first two, "On Suffering" and "On the Seriousness of Prayer," are of unknown provenance, but were probably written in Nazi Germany or during Heschel's London exile. Susannah Heschel recently discovered them among Heschel's private papers; to the best of our knowledge, they have never been published until now. The third, "On Dreaming God's Dream," was published in the *Bulletin* of New York's Congregation Habonim in September 1941. The last of the four meditations, "On Return," published in December 1939 in the newsletter of the Theodor Herzl Society in London, directly addresses the primary theme of this collection: the need to reclaim Jewish learning after the trauma of the destruction of European Jewry.

The teachings in this collection demonstrate Heschel's prescription for the future of the Jewish people in three ways. First, he teaches content: By writing about the Rabbinic period and the expulsion of the Jews from Spain and Portugal, Heschel introduces his audience to foundational chapters in their own story, about which some Jews have known little—Jews both in his time and ours. The essays on the Rabbis incorporate some of the most famous talmudic tales, stories that in another time and place had the character of shared family lore. Second, he creates connection: the particular struggles of the figures Heschel brings to light are parallel to the struggles faced during and after the destruction of European Jewry. And third, Heschel instructs through his methodology, exemplifying the revitalization of the tradition. In the words of his 1940 speech in London, he shows how "the content of Judaism's memory" can be "the educational material that nourishes us" in the present. Thus, in both content and form, these essays light the way for the Jews to whom falls the task of building a meaningful identity in the face of the destruction of the European Jewish community.

Heschel would grapple with the issue of effective Jewish education throughout his life. He concluded a 1953 article, based on an address to Jewish educators, with these words:

> A young man once wanted to become a blacksmith. So he became an apprentice to a blacksmith, and he learned all the necessary techniques of the trade—how to hold the tongs, how to lift the sledge, how to smite the anvil, even how to blow the fire with the

bellows. Having finished his apprenticeship, he was chosen to be employed at the smithery of the royal palace. However, the young man's delight soon came to an end, when he discovered that he had failed to learn how to kindle a spark. All his skill and knowledge in handling the tools were of no avail.

I am often embarrassed when I discover that I am myself like that apprentice—that I know facts and I know techniques, but I have failed to learn how to kindle a spark. I conclude, therefore, with the hope that you who work in the royal smithery of Jewish education will each of you be able to kindle a spark.[7]

His humility notwithstanding, Heschel's own work has proven him wrong: In these writings, and throughout his career, he has demonstrated over and over again what it means to kindle that spark.

EDITOR'S NOTE

The pieces in part 2 ("Personalities in Jewish History") and part 4 ("On the Jewish Holidays") were originally published in Berlin's Jewish press and did not include notes of any kind. The explanatory comments in those sections are ours, and we have included bibliographical endnotes identifying primary sources for the texts Heschel mentions.

In part 3 ("Don Yitzhak Abravanel"), Heschel included a set of mostly bibliographic notes. Our endnotes include his references to primary sources, sometimes slightly modified for consistency, along with additional bibliographic detail. His secondary sources—most of them in German—have not been included. In addition to some explanatory commentary of our own, we have included Heschel's occasional notes, identified as such. We have provided the translation of Hebrew titles, in brackets.

The translations in this volume are entirely our own, with two exceptions. First, parts of the translation of the Abravanel biography are based on an abridged translation by William Wolf published in the *Intermountain Jewish News Literary Supplement* on December 19, 1986. Second, in part 4 (For the Jewish Holidays in Berlin), the piece entitled "The Meaning of Repentance (Rosh Hashanah, 1936)" was first published in English translation in *Moral Grandeur and Spiritual Audacity*, edited by Susannah Heschel. We have made some minor changes to the translation.

IN THIS HOUR

PART 1

London

Jewish Learning in Exile

Context

Heschel arrived in London from Warsaw in July 1939—six weeks before Germany invaded Poland—on a transit visa and with a Polish passport that would soon be worthless. A job at the Hebrew Union College in Cincinnati was waiting for him, but he still lacked the visa that would enable him to enter and work in the United States. A more contingent status is difficult to imagine. The United Kingdom was taking in German and Austrian children desperate for shelter from Nazi persecution, but the British government's stance toward Jewish refugees was ambivalent at best. In May it had issued the white paper that signaled a sharp shift in British policy away from Zionist aspirations in Mandatory Palestine. When war broke out in September, immigration of refugees to the UK was cut radically. "Enemy aliens," including German and Austrian Jews, became subject to internment and deportation to Canada and Australia. For Heschel, England was a stopover, a place to wait for the precious U.S. visa.

But even as Heschel found himself in this most transitory of way stations, he embarked on a new project, driven by his remarkable energy, resilience, and sense of purpose. London, he wrote to Martin Buber, was a "spiritual desert," and he decided to use his time there, however long or short it would be, to establish a school for Jewish adult education, the Institute for Jewish Learning.

He brought the London institute to life under the umbrella of the Theodor Herzl Society, a Zionist organization with a largely Central European refugee membership. The society distributed a mimeographed newsletter, its *Mitteilungsblatt*, that promoted the institute both in anticipation of and subsequent to its opening in January 1940. The December 29 issue carried a short piece on the planned institute and identified Heschel as its academic director. Immediately preceding the announcement, on the first page, was an article by Heschel himself, entitled "Return."

Without mentioning the institute specifically, Heschel's piece is a clarion call for its task and its mission: "the pursuit of Jewish texts and shared learning, and the path to one's own Jewish life are a function of life, a question of Jews' being or not being." The article is included as the final piece in this collection.

The poster advertising the opening of the institute announced a roster of some nineteen lecturers, most of them scholars originally from Europe.[1] The first two weeks offered fifteen evening talks (some of them repeats), some in English, others in German, on topics such as "Readings of Easy Talmudic Texts," "Franz Rosenzweig," "Religious Movements in Palestine," "Letters as Witnesses to Jewish History," and Heschel's "Moses between God and Volk."[2] Listings for four subsequent semesters (through March 1942) offer some twenty-plus "public lectures" as well as three weekly seminars per semester, held in North London.

An announcement placed by the institute (and presumably penned by Heschel) in a British religious Zionist publication declares, "The Institute of Jewish Learning has been formed in response to the need of the times. Its aim is to foster the study of the sources of Jewish life and history and through this to foster a new Jewish spirit. The Institute for Jewish Learning is an independent, scientific institution."[3] The language here evokes some of Heschel's most important German educational experiences: calling the institution "scientific" likens it to Berlin's Hochschule für die Wissenschaft des Judentums; the emphasis on "sources" makes a connection with Frankfurt's Lehrhaus. The topics of the lectures and seminars were wide ranging. A representative sampling of their titles: "Racialism and Its Implications," "The Development of Jewish Art," "On Baruch

Spinoza," "The Jewish Interpretation of History," "The Psalms—A Book of Life," "Jews in English Literature," "Psychology of Refugees," "The Future of Hebrew Literature," "An Introduction to the Talmud," "The Spirit of Hebrew with Reference to the Kabbalah," "Reading of Maimonides," "Reading of Some Arabic Authors," "On Jewish Psychological Problems."

The timing of the institute's opening and Heschel's inaugural lecture on January 30 was oddly propitious: the following day he learned that his visa had been granted, removing the final hurdle to his entering the US. The following week's *Jewish Chronicle* reported on Heschel's talk: "There was a large audience when Professor S. Brodetsky and Dr. A. Heschel delivered their addresses last week at the opening of the Institute of Jewish Learning at Maccabi House. . . . Dr. Heschel gave an account of Jewish learning during the nineteenth and twentieth centuries. He expressed the view that all theories of education in the past failed, for they were ineffective in real life. What did keep Judaism alive up till today was the spirit which was not the possession but the destiny of Judaism. That realisation, he said, must be the aim of Jewish education."[4] Put differently: to be educated, in Heschel's words, is to become "bearers of the Spirit," where learning, "thinking in God's presence," is worship, is prayer.

Apparently not everyone in Heschel's audience approved of his assertion that learning is a religious act, and a piece in the Herzl Society's newsletter alludes to difficulties: "The first lecture of the Institute for Jewish Learning . . . made great demands on the willingness and ability of those listening to take it in."[5] In a February 7 letter to Martin Buber, Heschel candidly described the response to his talk: "My opening lecture, 'The Idea of Jewish Education' (which I, myself, think is good!), aroused indignation, because I put forth a uniquely Jewish idea of spiritual education. Those on the 'left' found it 'reactionary.' The ignorance and blindness of the people strikes me as the wonder of the century. I was a little annoyed. Others understood its implications."[6]

The address was intended for subsequent publication in England, but only a German typescript has been found. Embedded within the text are notes sketching a review of the evolution of Jewish education through a few hundred years of modern Jewish history—a lecture within a lecture whose pointed critique motivates the passion expressed in the main text. The notes illustrate that Heschel did not only speak about Jewish education, but also offered his listeners a rich lesson in Jewish history. They also present a precious, unguarded glimpse into Heschel's teacherly process. We have included these embedded lecture notes in a separate section, with some explanatory information to guide the reader.

The talk marked the opening of the London institute and the conclusion of Heschel's life in Europe. He had just turned thirty-three. On March 9, in Liverpool, he boarded the *Lancastria* for New York, a departure anticipated in his letter of the month before to Buber: "Now I will make my way to the sea and think of the sea of suffering in Poland."[7]

The Idea of Jewish Education

Heschel delivered this speech at the opening of the Institute for Jewish Learning in London, January 30, 1940. It has been translated from the manuscript "Die Idee der jüdischen Bildung" (Abraham Joshua Heschel Papers, box 280, folder 3, David M. Rubenstein Rare Book & Manuscript Library, Duke University Libraries, Durham, NC).

What is Jewish education? What is its essence, its value, its goal?

Does this century's prevailing ideal of human education correspond to the particular cultural condition of the Jews? Or is there a distinctively Jewish idea of education? What is its meaning? How can it be implemented?

I'm not thinking here of the specialists, who see their calling in research, but of the education that every Jew wants to have. What is a specifically Jewish education for the Jewish people?

That we must ask this question again despite our having such an ancient history of education is explained by the radical changes that occurred in Jewish life after the eighteenth century, flowing from Rabbi Israel Baal Shem in one direction and from Moses Mendelssohn in the other. To understand these changes we must have a sense of the condition of Jewish education in the main centers of Jewry in pre-Hasidic and pre-Mendelssohnian times, namely in Germany and in Poland. In the Jewish cultural understanding of the time, these two regions were one. People who were raised along the Vistula were appointed as rabbis along the Rhine and Main. Books that were conceived and written in Lithuania's melancholy landscape were published by Jewish printers in Bohemia and Moravia.

In this area of Jewish culture, where the medieval Jewish understanding of the world prevailed almost exclusively until the eighteenth century, the means and goals of education were clearly set. Educational activity consisted primarily in the study of the Babylonian Talmud and its commentaries. The Bible and postbiblical literature played a secondary role. The study of philosophical or kabbalistic writings was left to the very few.

The absolute sovereignty of this talmudic ideal no longer exists. But we have to account for the reasons that caused the Jews to surrender this ideal. The value of the Talmud did not shrivel only because of declining religiosity and alienation from the world of the sacred. In addition, other reasons lie in the talmudic ideal of education itself. The talmudists believed that all wisdom—not only the highest—could be found in the Talmud. But central themes of human knowledge, like the knowledge of nature, are not given any place in the Talmud. The exclusion of the sciences, which have had such a wonderful upsurge since the sixteenth century, stood in contrast to the ideal of some classical Talmud teachers, who had tried to stay on top of the educational developments of their time. This had to have negative consequences.[8] Further, the one-sidedness of the formalistic-legalistic way of thinking also caused the other directions of thought, the poetic, philosophical and philological, to suffer. The sophistication of the human mind is a result of modern human development, and the one-sided study of Talmud could not do it justice.

The need for intellectual freedom was another factor in this separation from the fixed system of the Talmud.

Another reason was the Aristotelian character of Talmud study. In order to attain a genuine command of talmudic writings and their way of thought, a correspondingly high degree of skill in logical thinking was necessary. This, however, could only be expected of the very few. Most people were not capable of it.

The leading authorities' most intense criticism was elicited by so-called *pilpul*. This was a technique for combining concepts that posed absolutely unreal, sophistic problems devoid of any halachic interest and tried to solve them by complicated logic. What mattered to the pilpulists was not so much truth and logical correctness as the beauty and originality of their conceptual combinations. Many regard *pilpul* as a degenerative form of talmudic thinking. [This is] a view, however, that will have to be revised one day.[9] In any case, the primacy of logic, the excessive emphasis on rational thinking, was one of the main reasons for the decline in Talmud study.[10]

There were times when talmudic education resulted in the overdevelopment of the intellect and the impoverishment of other abilities and talents. Often it led to an overvaluation of erudition and to a prejudice favoring contemplation over moral and aesthetic values. In fact, this kind of degeneration occurred again and again, as did resistance to it.

Here the manuscript contains notes for a review of the prevailing trends in Jewish education over the preceding centuries: Hasidism, *Wissenschaft des Judentums* (Science of Judaism), and the Eastern European Haskalah (Jewish Enlightenment) (see page 19).

In recent years we have come to know the ignominy of human beings. We have experienced their metamorphosis into brutal barbarians. And we ask ourselves: how was this metamorphosis possible? Let us not forget that this happened among a people that occupied an important position in Western culture and education. Here the "promise of potential" has been accomplished. These people can read and write, make music and draw, describe nature and practice crafts. They possess a sense of order and of duty, a talent for organization and a gift for public speaking. But apparently this educational ideal has missed its mark. Apparently human beings cannot be trusted, and we must not abandon them to the demonic that lives within them. And it is the fundamental task of our life to work on the person himself. How much energy we spend in constructing a car with absolute precision, and yet how minimal, indeed almost negligible, are our efforts to form the inner person. And what is the goal of working on people? In this terrible crisis of Western culture that question virtually determines our destiny.

Often the goal of working on the person is intended to develop a sense for values, for the good, the beautiful, and the true. But we often overlook the fact that people also tend to pursue other values, like power and wealth, etc. In Georg Simmel[11] we find the formulation that a person is educated "whose objective knowledge has been integrated into the vitality of his subjective development and existence."[12] This thought, too, although it contains an important idea, leads in a false direction. The fallacy in all these theories of education is that they are psychological, that is, that they base the essence of education on one's inner ability, that it finds no purchase for the continuation of that education external to the individual. But the inner life of the modern person is so chaotic that no foundation for a temple can be supported in it. In the witches' cauldron of a person's drives, resentments, and complexes, whatever insights and understanding he has gained and digested can become the ingredients for a devil's meal.

Another error in this theory of education is that it atomizes the individual and separates him from all that connects him to the world in which he lives. All living things can only be understood in the context in which they exist. The characteristics of animals, the meaning of biological functions, the course of electromagnetic processes can only be understood and interpreted within the environment where they exist or occur. We can understand the biological and physiological processes of the human organism only by keeping in mind its place in its surroundings, its environment, in the widest sense. It would be impossible to describe the digestive process without simultaneously considering the continual climatic and atmospheric interactions and the character of the nutrients themselves.

And so, too, the process of education can only be completely understood if we consider it in the context in which it belongs. What, precisely, is this context in which we stand as humans? There is such a context. There is no dearth of signs or proofs for such a context. We list here only a few of them: society, history, of which our generation is but a tiny part; death, to which our life submits itself; and above all the knowledge that man is

9

not alone in the cosmos, the knowledge that he is neither the master of the world, nor master of his own life.

Left to his own devices, man reveals himself as a bundle of drives. Left to his own devices, he becomes an animal. Even reason isn't able to preserve his dignity. He willingly becomes degraded to a creature of drives that knows nothing more than its libido, to a creature that knows no freedom and is the slave of material or social factors. It has finally reached the point where one can no longer distinguish a human from other living beings.

The Biblical Answer

We are guided by only one essential characteristic: that we are made in God's image, the highest attribute that has ever been claimed for man. What is the meaning of our being made in God's image? What is the highest attribute of man? Wherein lies the analogy to God? In the relationship to Spirit.

What is Spirit? To give a universal characterization of Spirit is a task compared to which the squaring of the circle would be trivial. Here we want to characterize only the essential feature of the biblical understanding of Spirit. Here it is. Biblical thought calls Spirit that which moves God, what concerns Him or comes from Him.

Man does not experience God as static or eternal but as dynamic. There is *motion* in God as if He were moved by the life of beings. Man's deeds concern Him, from the point of view of good and evil. God is more than Spirit, but it is His Spirit that man is able to experience.

The content residing in this Spirit is expressed in the instructions and speeches of the prophets. Its primary qualities are: oneness, truth, justice, and holiness. To work on a person in the Jewish sense means to place the person before the reality of the Spirit, enabling him to participate in a constant and vital engagement with the Spirit.

In the first chapter of Genesis we read: The Spirit hovered over the water. To this the Talmud comments: "The Spirit hovered like a dove over its young, without touching them."[13] As humans became part of nature, the Spirit was removed from them. It hovers over them, but doesn't touch them. Never was the Spirit more distant than it is today. The task of Judaism in this interaction—and its true help to the nations—is to make the voice of the Spirit speak.

To be close to the Spirit means to be moved by that which moves God, to be in sympathy with God. From God's perspective, what is valuable in the world is spiritual. We approach the Spirit when we enter into relationship with ultimate questions. To live spiritually means to be affected and moved, endowed and challenged. By learning about good and evil, by struggling with the truth, we increase our strength for participation in Spirit.

People resist the effects and the movements of the Spirit. In a crisis, however, when all confidence in oneself has been shaken, they are sometimes more receptive to the movements of the Spirit. But no attitude is as suitable for this experience as the peace that comes from fidelity to the meaning of the world.

There are two kinds of relationship to the Spirit. One is that of participation. As people, we have Spirit as a possession that we can command, and also relinquish.

For Jews, Spirit is destiny. This means that the Spirit has mastery over us, and that which happens to us follows from our relationship to Spirit. Spirit works in our history as an independent power that determines our existence and our will. We were preserved neither by blood nor earth, neither money nor the state but by Spirit. But we have the choice. We can also shake off the yoke, and then we are no longer subject to the power of the Spirit but come instead under the sway of other powers.

The urge to continue to develop the spirit of Judaism, the appropriation of its values and insights, their incorporation into the structure of the soul—this was the deepest desire of our fathers. Not the completed form, not the striving to become, themselves, an artwork, but priestly service in the worship of the Spirit, serving, sacrificing, increasing the magnificence of the Spirit. The greatest bliss a Jew could experience was the Spirit. The *unio mystica* with God is foreign to Judaism. The Jewish experience was union with the Torah.

What is the purpose of Jewish education? Reading texts is not an end unto itself. [They are not merely] educational materials or literature. It does not mean using Jewish libraries, and researching in archives.

The purpose of educational work is: (1) to maintain and enrich Judaism's memory, and (2) to enable the individual to participate in this memory. What does that mean?

Not only the individual, but the community, too, possesses a memory. The power of that memory is also a measure of the strength of our culture. The ideas and experiences that we were granted over the course of our long history have not been forgotten. The memory of our people has preserved these ideas. Independently of what we knew and what we wished, these ideas were carried forth. The storing of the Spirit, the content of Judaism's memory, is the educational material that nourishes us. What has been written down into books is like the body. The soul exists only in the act of transmission. The books are only signs, notes. It is the aliveness of the Jew that makes music from it.

The Spirit we are talking about is intimately interwoven with its bearer, with the Jewish community. It is borne by the Jews. This means that in this relationship Israel is both the bearer and the Spirit that is borne. They depend on one another for their existence. That is the meaning of the transmitted tradition of the Jews, the living interpretation of the eternal teaching.

A Jew must be aware of this if he wants to come to clarity in his relationship with God. For us, Jewish literature is not a dead past but the immediate present.

We are not indebted to the archaeologists for the biblical writings that we read today. They did not first have to be excavated like a collapsed temple out of the rubble of antiquity. Ever since they were written down, throughout our entire history, we have stood in engagement with them. We approach them differently than we do, for example, the old Egyptian hymns. There is something in us that answers when we are seized by the words of our literature. To the Jew it sometimes seems as if a memory is being awakened in him.

The voice of the Spirit speaks from those whose thoughts grow out of a shared memory of Judaism, and our historical experiences are at work in their decisions. It is silent when one speculates arbitrarily. Participation in the Jewish spirit is accomplished as recollection. Only from our memory can we think as Jews. Our responsibility is to maintain the memory and to transmit them.

Participating in memory means that the thoughts in Jewish writing become elements in our judgments, motivations for our actions, measures for our thinking. This path leads through the recognition that one belongs to Judaism not biologically or racially but spiritually. We acknowledge that we are a part of the Spirit of Judaism and take the Jewish people's memory into ourselves. We do not reach the goal if we view the values of the Spirit from above—historically, sociologically, psychologically or homiletically. As long as there is that kind of distance between Spirit and life, there is no mutual fertilization. Incorporating the words of the Spirit into the order of daily life. Making the words into intimate factors of our lives. The Spirit should become a part of us, become spontaneous.

The vital sources of Jewish education are not the books but the people, the bearers of memory. The essence of education is not in the letters, but in those who engage with the Spirit and bear witness to it. The duty of Judaism is to educate the Jews to be bearers of that which has been passed down. Being educated means to be bearers of the Spirit. Without a living tradition, as Jews we would go under. This is why the break with the tradition is so dangerous to our survival.

One thing is clear: education is not identical to knowledge. Education means formation, education shapes the person. But the fact that one possesses knowledge is not a sign that someone has been formed. Education is not a thing but a process, an act. Education *happens* to a person.

The Jews call the happening of education *learning*. The commandment to learn is not the demand for a certain quantity of knowledge or a number of catechism articles. Not the product, but learning itself is what matters. Learning is a service in and of itself.

Determining a Specifically Jewish Idea of Education on the Basis of an Analysis of the Old Jewish Form of Education

What was the meaning of learning Talmud? The interest in Talmud wasn't scholarly; the appropriation of knowledge was not its main purpose. Its purpose was the learning itself. One learned because of interest in religion; one learned because it was a commandment to concern oneself with Torah. Thus learning became a matter of worship and took on priestly features.

At first this seems surprising. After all, talmudic texts consist primarily of speculative discussions, logical operations in law, and differentiation of concepts: a rather dry content. Isn't it paradoxical that a significant part of Jewish religiosity was spent in such an intellectual activity?

Even today, there are a considerable number of people who devote themselves to the study of Talmud and undertake it as a religious activity. And yet it is not the knowledge of the law and its practical applicability that constitutes the religious meaning of this study. Nor is it to suppress the noise of the everyday and escape into the speculative world of talmudic thought. The decisive factor was the inner value of talmudic thinking itself.

Talmudic thought was sacred thinking whose value lay not in its logical correctness but in its metaphysical origin. In the words of an old saying: Whatever a diligent student will innovate in the future was already said to Moshe at Sinai.[14]

Perhaps it was the intellectual imitation of divine thinking on which the magic of Talmud study was built. He who studied Talmud was aware that it was as if the interpretations and explanations of a dark passage in the Talmud, the solution to a controversial problem, were of concern to the Eternal One or were once present in God's Spirit. Sometimes one believed in having experienced God's help in the search for a solution. To some degree, something of this way of thinking was alive in the awareness of every sincere student of Talmud. Those who were not able to penetrate into the depths of talmudic thought, who could therefore not experience the Talmud by thinking actively, treasured the feeling of being close to revealed holy words. To be present in the sphere of truth and purity meant to stand in the radiant field of a metaphysical light. This experience was made possible by the participation of the entire person. Not only reason but also the soul participated in study. And the soul was also pulled in by the power of the music, by the Talmud-*niggun* that with sweetness and forcefulness captured one's feelings in an infinite net and introduced the student of Talmud, when he gave himself up entirely to its thinking, into a beautifully noble world. For even the secular, practical legal cases that are treated in the Talmud are like dreams: the topic may be from everyday life, but it is woven from a different cloth.

Thinking about the Torah was experienced as thinking with God. Learning is thinking in God's presence, sinking into God's Spirit. Many will think it strange when we characterize the absorption into a talmudic speculation about problems pertaining to restitution for damages as *prayer*. But that's how it was, and still is today. This ability to experience learning as prayer: that is the essence of the Jewish Spirit. Jewish education is the ability to interact with the Spirit.

In the essays of Francis Bacon that were published in 1597 with the title *Meditations Sacrae*, we find the sentence "Ipsa scientia potestas est." The English translation, which appeared in 1598, reads, "For knowledge itself is power."

Knowledge Is Power

This is propaganda on behalf of Haskalah [Enlightenment],[15] furthering education with this argument.

Power is the ability to bend other beings to one's own will. It was the dream of some thinkers to spiritualize power. By means of this equation, Spirit became power.

Everyone agreed that power was desirable, but without knowing what one would use it for. People forgot that power without Spirit is the monopoly of demons. And so, betraying the Spirit, one surrendered to the demons, the uncanny powers that destroy all that is good: life, freedom, dignity and truth. This world without Spirit falls apart. The catastrophe has begun.

Anyone who might have the courage to proclaim that the essence of things is the will to attain Spirit would be mocked. But the pathological cry that the will to power is the essence of all things was taken up by millions and now entire nations are raised according to this axiom.

To direct one's life toward power is to devalue that which is essential in a person. For humanity's essence is to strive toward values, and over values there is no mastery. The path to values, to peace, and to the integrity of the individual is through love.

All love is a relationship to values, a relationship to what is valuable. The beloved is always loved for his quality, for the sake of that which is valuable in him. We love a being when we feel ourselves pulled in to the values that exist in him.

There is a sentence in Aristotle's Metaphysics that says, "God moves the world as the beloved moves the lover." This is also the meaning of learning, to be moved by that which is of the Spirit, to find joy in the existence of the Spirit, to love the Spirit.

In the language of the Bible, the Hebrew word *yada* יד, which refers to the concept of knowledge, is also used to mean both knowledge and the act of love. *Yada* יד means not only knowledge through reason, but the most intimate interaction with things. It means knowing things lovingly.

What matters is not the extent of the acquired knowledge, but that one recognizes values: the truth, the good, the beautiful. Learning must be directed to this goal. Learning should be an act that is valuable in and of itself. It should be an interaction with the object, interested in experiencing its form, its content, and its meaning.

In the face of the assertion: "Knowledge is power," Judaism must proclaim, "Knowledge is love."

Notes for a Lecture on Jewish Education in the Modern Era

What follows are Heschel's notes, sometimes fragmentary, on prevailing trends in Jewish education. Our endnotes are designed to help the reader fill in the gaps. The despair Heschel voices as this review concludes sets the tone for the second half of his London talk.

Reform of Education by the Hasidim[16]

Maimonides[17]

Giving preference to applied material: Study of the *Shulhan Aruch*. Creation of the *Shulhan Aruch HaRav*. Education of workmen and rural Jews.[18]

Giving preference to the *aggadah* [and] *Zohar*: Freedom. Imagination. Feeling.[19]

Creation of myth: The Hasidic tale.[20]

Personality of the teacher as role model. Hasidic exegesis—*al derech ha-avodah*—"in the way of service."[21]

Abstract acumen of the *drosh*—"interpretation."

Profundity of meditations on life and the formation of the soul.[22]

Weaknesses

No engagement with the culture of the time.

Immediate environment—no culture.

Not consistent in implementation. Fear of opposition.

Neglect of the culture of forms, of language.

Wissenschaft des Judentums [Science of Judaism][23]

The breakdown of the old culture. Flight into philology and the study of antiquity. Neglect of philosophy.

Science/academic scholarship as an aid to emancipation.

"Rehabilitation of Judaism, to effect its integration as an equal participant in the world history of the spirit." (Wiener)[24]

Good reputation among the Jews themselves.

Due to canonization of the Talmud text, personal freedom suffers.[25]

Geiger: not rigidly immutable.[26]

History, which is still decisive today. Criticism.

Eduard Meyer calls it "the greatest task of historical study . . . to understand what has taken place as taking place, thinking oneself into the moment where what we perceive as historical fact had not yet happened, but was still to happen, still to be born."[27]

"The true origins of both physical and spiritual life remain an unfathomable mystery to human reflection and thought." (Burdach)[28]

In the East

Against talmudic education arises Jewish Enlightenment, called *Haskalah*. It was primarily about reform in education, not about religion. The significance of education.[29]

The goals of Enlightenment were: to free the Jews intellectually from the ghetto and spread among them the general education of the time. Its further goals were: the elevation of a Hebrew style that had fallen into neglect, schooling in secular subjects, turning

to the Bible and away from the Talmud. European
education was the light. The Enlightenment—*bat
hashamayim*, "the daughter of heaven." Pathos.[30]
The secularization of education. Yiddish schools.
Hebrew schools. The discovery of language.[31]

Environment

Changes in educational ideals. Always spiritual
motivations.

According to [Immanuel] Kant (1724–1804) "the perfection of the species is the secret [aim] that stands
behind all education." "Through education man
shall become a better man." (Fischer)[32] Alternatively,
humanity: the fulfillment of man's essence.

But what is "a better man?" Changes in this concept.

Kalos kagathos: Greek educational ideal.[33]

Gentleman: English educational ideal. Perfected control
over the body, proud self-confidence, a balanced
disposition.

The humanistic ideal of education of Wilhelm von
Humboldt,[34] which was valid in the nineteenth
century, strives for a free, manifold and beautiful
unfolding of man's potential.

Also the naturalistic pedagogy of the second half of
the nineteenth century had the slogan "Unfolding
of the natural potential in humanity" as the goal
of education.

Are all natural potentials good? Unfolding to what end?

Nineteenth century. Development of knowledge.
Educational monopoly of one social stratum. An

acquired external polish. Good deportment—internally rotten. A sense of order is cultivated, but order in the soul isn't a concern. No culture of soul. Psychoanalysis—the only access to the sacred.

Collapse

Most recent tendency: Sociology gives the norms for pedagogy. The idea of community. Not the formation of a person's essence.

Moloch: Volk[35]

Nineteenth century: Destruction of the personality. Division of labor. Productivity. Eduard Spranger calls for educating people to the personal awareness of power.[36]

National Socialist education: the fundamental cultivation of race, and the consciously völkisch education on the basis of a conception of the world to which all members of the community are bound.[37]

Spengler rejects the work of education altogether: "If I have taught the people how to weave a good basket I've done more for their education than all the adult education programs."[38] A nation for whom this norm becomes the practice will, in fewer than twenty years, devolve into slavery and serfdom. Hatred of the Spirit means the collapse of human dignity in the hands of those who cannot bear it in themselves or tolerate it in others. Freedom becomes a person's need through his relationship to Spirit. When a person becomes degraded, a beast of burden, or a tool, that need disappears.

Poland: The secularization of education that was the
idol of the Jewish Enlightenment, in Berlin as well
as in Odessa, has lost its purpose in recent years.
The void.
The dream of academic education ceases.
Profanation of the universities in Germany and in
Poland.
Youth without an educational goal.

PART 2

Personalities in Jewish History

Context

Heschel's "Personalities" essays are based mostly on stories from the Talmud, rewoven to create a continuous narrative. For the reader who will find it helpful, we offer an overview of the relevant historical period, as well as some explanations of terms.

These essays are set in the mishnaic period, encompassing the first quarter of the first millennium CE, the early centuries of the Rabbinic era. With the destruction of the Second Temple in 70 CE, a social structure based on a cult of animal sacrifice, led by a hereditary priesthood and tied to a particular place, eventually gave way to a culture based on law and text, led by scholars of law and text, and portable to any place where laws and texts could travel. Heschel traces this transformation from the fall of the Temple through the production of the Mishnah.

The Mishnah presents the Jewish traditions and practices of the period as a set of propositions and debates. It was codified in the hope that it would become a legal and literary structure that could replace the physical structure of the Temple as the center of Jewish communal life. Indeed, it is the core text around which the Talmud is built and the first text beyond the Bible to become an essential part of the foundation of Judaism.

Heschel reflects on this period through his portrayal of eight mishnaic sages. The first and seventh figures, Rabbi Johanan ben Zakkai and Rabbi Judah Hanasi, are often used to represent the two endpoints of the mishnaic period, from about 70 CE to about 200 CE. With his eighth "personality" Heschel goes a step further, showing that the Mishnah was incomplete and that its codification was just a starting point. He gives final pride of place to a lesser-known figure, Rabbi Hiyya, a post-mishnaic sage who died around 230 CE. In Heschel's presentation, Rabbi Hiyya destabilizes the happy ending implied by the codification of the Mishnah and, in so doing, points the way toward the unfolding of the talmudic era.

The central issues at play in the first and second centuries CE were like those that had plagued Jewish society for centuries: the relationship between the Jews and foreign powers who conquered them, the resulting internal conflicts among the Jews, and the pressures historical developments brought to bear on the Jewish religion. In 587–586 BCE the Babylonians had conquered Judea, ending the rule of the Davidic monarchy and destroying the First Temple, where priests descended from the line of Aaron had presided over the Israelite sacrificial rites for four hundred years. Then, after only a few decades, the Persians conquered Babylonia and allowed the Jews to rebuild their Temple, but for two centuries Judea was a client state of Persia. In 332 BCE Alexander the Great conquered Judea, inaugurating an era in which Greek culture permeated every aspect of social, political, and material life. Alexander died eleven years later, but the region remained under Hellenistic rule until 168 BCE, when the Maccabees led a revolt against the foreign rulers and the more assimilated Jews.

The Hasmonean dynasty introduced by the Maccabees lasted less than a century. It was the only period in which the Jews had sustained political control over the region from the time of the Babylonian conquest in 587 BCE until the establishment of the modern State of Israel in 1948. After a few generations, the Hasmonean dynasty devolved into fratricidal disarray, paving the way for the Roman conquest in 63 BCE. Throughout the Second Temple period the role of client state was a familiar one for the Jews: they were ruled first by the Babylonians, then by the Persians, then by the Greeks, and finally by the Romans.

In the first centuries of the Common Era, governance of Judea was in the hands of Roman administrators. At first, providing that the Jews collected taxes and turned them over to the Roman authorities, they were allowed sufficient autonomy within their community. But eventually taxes were increased and the authorities became more intrusive and harsher in their treatment of the Jews. Roman cruelty, corruption, and incompetence led to disastrous economic failure and intensified Jewish unrest.

The discontent in the Jewish community added heat to factional divisions that had long simmered. There was disagreement over the importance of political sovereignty: was it essential that the region be ruled in accordance with Jewish law, even if that meant war, or was it sufficient that the Jews were permitted to follow their laws and customs in individual, family, and communal life? There was disagreement about the nature of Jewish law: was it to be derived solely from the written Torah, or should it include traditions passed down from earlier generations, even when they had no clear relationship with the canonical text? And there was disagreement about assimilation: all factions were influenced by Greek and Roman culture, but what was the value of these cultural influences, and where were the appropriate limits?

Finally, in 66 CE militant Jews who believed in the centrality of Jewish political power staged an armed rebellion against Roman rule. There were some early victories, but it wasn't long before the Roman general Vespasian, sent in by the Emperor Nero to quash the rebellion, had recaptured everything but Jerusalem. When Nero died, Vespasian's attention was distracted by his plot to succeed Nero as emperor, and he put his son Titus in charge of finishing off the Jewish rebellion. For many months, the Romans held Jerusalem under siege, and inside its walls the Jews were killing each other in sectarian violence.

Heschel's first essay, on Rabbi Johanan ben Zakkai, begins here. Heschel likens Rabbi Johanan to the prophet Jeremiah who, in the sixth century, urged the Jews not to rebel against their Babylonian conquerors. Political redemption, proclaimed Jeremiah, was in the hands of God, and until God's chosen moment arrived, Jewish survival might require submission to foreign overlords. In the sixth century BCE, continued resistance did indeed lead to complete destruction, as Jeremiah had predicted. With that earlier tragedy in mind, Rabbi Johanan was willing to look for a way to coexist with the Romans—which put him at odds with other Jewish groups, particularly the party known as the Zealots. The Zealots also believed the redemption of the Jews was at stake, but they saw the process differently. They were the most prominent of a number of groups who expected the imminent arrival of the Jewish Messiah and believed that it was incumbent on the Jews to hasten that arrival by fighting the foreign powers with zeal, even against all odds.

Rabbi Johanan was proven right: the rebellion of the Jews ended in disaster, culminating with the destruction of the Second Temple in 70 CE. In his essay on Rabbi Johanan ben Zakkai, Heschel points to messianism as one of the factors behind the tragically false hopes of the misguided fighters. When the fall of Masada in 73 CE ended the last stand of the Jewish rebels, the Roman victory was complete.

In the ensuing decades, under the emperors Trajan and Hadrian, oppression only got worse. In 132, a charismatic leader known as Shimon Bar Kochba launched a second rebellion against Rome. Historical and talmudic sources show that his original name was Shimon Bar Kosiba—the nickname "Bar Kochba," meaning "son of a star," reflected the messianic hopes pinned on him and on his goal of reclaiming Jerusalem and restoring the Temple. The Romans crushed the Bar Kochba revolt in 135 CE, then punished the perpetrators harshly: many were executed, many were deported, and Jewish practice was effectively outlawed. Rabbi Akiba was among those martyred in this bloody aftermath. To complete the process of removing the Jewish stamp from the region, Jerusalem was renamed Aelia Capitolina, and Judea became Palestina, or Palestine. Any remaining Jewish hope that the Temple would soon be restored was extinguished. Again, Heschel points to messianism as the culprit—this time it was Rabbi Akiba who was swept up in its fervor.

Hadrian died in 138, shortly after the defeat of Bar Kochba, and the next emperor, Antonius Pius, rescinded the harshest of the Hadrianic decrees. Jews were still not permitted to live in Jerusalem, but they were allowed to study Torah and engage in Jewish practice elsewhere in Palestine. However, many influential Jewish scholars and leaders had emigrated during the persecutions and had joined established exilic communities in Babylonia and elsewhere. Even though it was now possible to return to the Holy Land, many chose to remain in the diaspora and retain leadership roles there. Some questioned the assumption that the voice of the Palestinian Jewish leaders was more authoritative than that of the diasporic rabbis. The essay on Rabbi Shimon ben Gamliel II, set in this period, portrays this power conflict as it affected the reestablishment of Palestine as the center of Jewish culture, law, and institutional leadership.

Leadership: The Sanhedrin, the Prince, and the Patriarch

Under Roman rule, governance of the Jewish community was in the hands of a body known as the "Sanhedrin"—from the Greek word *synedrion*, meaning "sitting together." Scholars debate the precise function and makeup of the Sanhedrin in Second Temple times, but generally agree that it was a judicial body serving the high priest, meeting in the temple precincts to adjudicate religious and civil law. Traditional Jewish sources describe it as an assembly of seventy-one: a pair of leaders called *nasi* (literally "prince," sometimes translated "president") and *av beit din* (literally "father of the court," sometimes translated "vice president"), plus sixty-nine sages.

The last of the pairs to lead the Sanhedrin while the Temple stood were Hillel and Shammai, whose partnership extended from about 30 BCE until Hillel's death around 10 CE. Shammai continued as *nasi* for two decades. Hillel's grandson, Gamliel I, succeeded him, and Gamliel's son, Shimon ben Gamliel I, followed in succession, inaugurating the Hillelite family dynasty that would be central to Palestinian Jewish leadership for three centuries.

Shimon ben Gamliel I died during the revolt of 66 to 73 CE, as the Romans quashed the first Jewish rebellion. With the fall of the Temple and the dissolution of the priesthood, both the physical and the sociopolitical context for the Sanhedrin ceased to exist. As legend has it, it was Heschel's first "personality," Johanan ben Zakkai, who created the context in which a new version of the Sanhedrin would come to be. While the battle still raged, he faked his own death and had himself smuggled out of the besieged city in order to escape the wrath of the Jewish extremists who would have preferred to see him dead than engaging in détente with the Romans. He managed to get the ear of the Roman general, and he negotiated for permission to run a house of study, to be set up in Yavne near the Mediterranean coast, far from the devastation of Jerusalem. The sages who gathered there would develop the culture of law and learning in which the new Judaism would grow.

Around 80 CE, when the war was over and the Jewish defeat sealed, a new Sanhedrin was formed, meeting not in Jerusalem but in Yavne. It was a revolutionary idea: a Sanhedrin with no connection to the Temple or the high priesthood, a Sanhedrin whose authority was conferred by its association with the house of study. On the other hand, the choice of a *nasi* was designed to maintain continuity with the past.

The first three Rabbis to be officially appointed *nasi* in the post-temple Sanhedrin brought the Hillelite family dynasty back to its leadership role. They are among the subjects of Heschel's essays: Rabbi Gamliel II, his son, Rabbi Shimon ben Gamliel II, and Shimon's son, Rabbi Judah Hanasi. The traditional claim that this line of leaders was descended from Hillel who, in turn, was descended from King David[1] may have been folkloric, but it had a profound consequence: it suggested that the new leadership was vested with dignity and authority whose antiquity and luster was even greater than that of the high priests of the Second Temple, stretching all the way back to the Davidic monarchy.

The Romans endowed the *nasi* with even more legitimacy by also assigning him the role of Patriarch—from the Greek, meaning "father(land) ruler." The Patriarch was the point of contact between the Roman rulers and the Jews. He was responsible for internal governance and tax collection. Heschel refers to the *nasi* sometimes as "prince" and sometimes as "patriarch." Both terms designate the same person: the first as the leader facing inward toward the Jewish community, the second as the representative facing outward toward Rome.[2]

Written and Oral Law

Heschel uses the terms "Oral Law" and "Oral Teaching" to describe the non-scriptural Jewish traditions that were being developed, codified, and written down in this period. The acceptance of these traditions as central elements of religious law played a major role in defining Rabbinic Judaism. The story of the maturation of the Oral Law and the leadership consensus to accept it is an important subplot that stretches across all eight essays.

The story begins in the Second Temple period, when the question of the relative importance of Torah and non-scriptural traditions was among the issues that divided Jews politically and religiously. Various sects—subgroups that were in some ways like political parties and in other ways like religious communities—held opposing positions on the subject. In particular, the Sadducees believed that the Written Law—the Torah that was understood to have been revealed to Moses and written by his hand—constituted the entirety of Jewish law. Their rivals, the Pharisees, supplemented the written Torah with traditions passed down from teachers to students that extended and molded the law over time—traditions they understood to be as important as the Torah itself. Simply to call these traditions "Oral Law" amounted to a partisan claim.

The conflict about the relative importance of Torah and tradition ran parallel to a conflict about the relative importance of priests and ordinary Israelites. Hand in hand with the idea that the written text was the sole carrier of Jewish law came the conviction that the activity of the priests was the central element of Jewish life. The oral traditions, by contrast, tended to increase the relevance of Jewish law outside the Temple. For example, the Torah abounds with rules about temple sacrifices and sacred food donations to support the priests, as well as stringent requirements for ritual purity incumbent on the priests who offered the sacrifices and consumed the sacred food. The Oral Law extended the reach of those rules so that some of them became relevant not only to priests but to every Israelite, affecting their own kitchens and marriage beds. This law was the province of sages who learned and taught in study houses and academies, not of priestly families who attended to ritual sacrifices. It is no accident that the Oral Law came into its own in the generation following the destruction of the Temple, when the priestly role became largely irrelevant.

Rabbinic Literature: Midrash, Mishnah, Tosefta, and Talmud

The term "Rabbi" refers to the sages who studied and taught the Oral Law, and the record of their work is Rabbinic literature: midrash, Mishnah, Tosefta, and Talmud, all terms Heschel uses in these essays. Over the course of history, the culture of learning that Rabbi Johanan ben Zakkai inaugurated in Heschel's first essay came to be based as much on these texts as on the Bible. Heschel's Rabbis are at once creators of and characters in these texts.

The work of the house of study was centered on the Oral Law—holding on to the received traditions, reciting the varied opinions of the various sages, collecting and organizing their sayings into forms that could more easily be remembered and repeated—but not at the expense of the Written Law. The genre of biblical interpretation known as midrash functioned to ground the Oral Law in the Torah, showing how verses of the Bible could be opened up to reveal hidden references to apparently unrelated legal traditions. Midrash too was part of the Oral Law, and its study and dissemination were so important that the house of study was called a *beit midrash*—literally, "a house of midrash." Heschel presents Rabbi Akiba as the great genius of midrash: " [T]hat the Oral Teaching is inherent in the Bible was Rabbi Akiba's seminal thought. Through the virtuosic artistry of his interpretations he was able to discover the one inside the other."

Midrash was collected and recorded in anthologies in ancient times, though the precise dating of both the collections and their contents is a subject of scholarly debate. Midrash provided a bridge between the Written and the Oral Law and helped to build trust in the authenticity of the latter. But midrash gives precedence to Torah: the orally transmitted laws and traditions were expressed, remembered—and eventually recorded—in the order of the biblical verses, as commentary on those verses.

The text whose production is the denouement of Heschel's story is the Mishnah, redacted circa 200 CE by Heschel's seventh "personality," Rabbi Judah Hanasi. In a few centuries this text would become the core of the Talmud. In contrast with midrash, the Mishnah gives precedence to the content of the Oral Law. It is organized by subject, like a law code, and while it includes some midrashic commentary, it is not concerned to demonstrate that each of its claims is grounded in the Bible.

The Mishnah is organized by topic into sixty sections grouped into six divisions.[3] Often it lays out a set of varying opinions in the names of various Rabbis. Often, but not always, it is clear which is the majority viewpoint and which are dissenting minority positions. There is rarely any attempt to sort out who is right and who is wrong. The text uses a distinctive literary style, full of symmetry and parallelism, which may have helped with memorization in the years when its parts were transmitted orally. The opinions of about 180 sages are quoted, prominent among them Heschel's first seven personalities.

The Mishnah contains only a portion of the transmitted traditions on each topic. Many more conversations and positions were remembered and repeated in the study houses and academies than were recorded by its collator, Rabbi Judah Hanasi. There is no record of the criteria by which statements were selected for inclusion, and those that were omitted are also considered important and authoritative. Remembered traditions that are not included in the Mishnah are called *baraitot* (singular: *baraita*), literally, "outside things," and the most organized and extensive collection of them is the Tosefta.

The Tosefta uses the same organizational scheme as the Mishnah. The contents also overlap, sometimes matching, sometimes contradicting, sometimes adding new material or attributing statements differently. Contemporary scholars debate its authorship. Heschel, in agreement with the traditional sources, ascribes the Tosefta to his eighth and last "personality," Rabbi Hiyya, and his disciple, Oshaiah.

The learning in the houses of study over the centuries following the codification of the Mishnah generated a second layer of the Oral Law: the Gemara. The Gemara contains a vast variety of material reflecting the free-flowing conversations in the houses of study. Its contents are sometimes described as belonging to two subgenres: *halachah*—legal material—and *aggadah*—stories and folklore, sometimes about the Rabbis and their lives, sometimes about life under Roman rule. Together, the Mishnah and the Gemara make up the Talmud, which was committed to writing between 450 and 600 CE. Present-day twenty-volume editions of the Talmud fill nearly six thousand pages.

Except for Rabbi Hiyya, the subjects of Heschel's essays lived in the time of the Mishnah, and their opinions on traditions and legal matters are recorded there. But the lore about their lives that informs Heschel's personality studies is drawn almost entirely from the Gemara—snapshots passed down from their students to the students of their students. It is not so much history as ancestral memory.

In its legal discussions the Gemara often returns to the methods of midrash to explore the biblical grounding for apparently ungrounded statements in the Mishnah. But perhaps the most characteristic moving force of Talmud is the work of comparing and attempting to harmonize the sayings of the Mishnah with *baraitot* that seem to contradict them. It is the tension created by differences and gaps in received traditions that provides the energy for the constant dialogue that spreads from the pages of the Talmud through layers of later commentary and into the study halls of the contemporary Jewish world. By extending his series to include Rabbi Hiyya, Heschel sets the stage for the ongoing cycle of codification and dissent that will become an engine of the Jewish culture of learning for millennia.

Rabbi Johanan ben Zakkai

Heschel's first "Personalities" essay opens in Jerusalem around 70 CE, during the Jewish revolt against Roman occupation, just before the fall of the Second Temple. Some Jews saw Johanan ben Zakkai's attempt to find a working equilibrium with the Romans as traitorous, but according to Rabbinic lore, his negotiations were responsible for saving the remnant that allowed Judaism to survive.

In the course of the essay Heschel connects Johanan ben Zakkai with two biblical figures: Jeremiah and Ezra. In the book of Jeremiah, set before the fall of the First Temple, the prophet warns against the danger of military arrogance in the face of an occupying power. In the books of Ezra and Nehemiah, set in the fifth century BCE after the Israelites returned from the Babylonian exile, Ezra defines the form and content of communal Torah reading. By likening Johanan ben Zakkai's innovations to those of Ezra, Heschel suggests that they were as weighty as Torah itself, and that the "moral and spiritual recovery" they offered was similarly profound.

This essay was first published in the *Gemeindeblatt der jüdischen Gemeinde zu Berlin* on February 23, 1936.

The immense Roman catapults hurled massive stones into the holy city and breached its fortifications. Houses collapsed under the weight of the troops standing on the roofs,[4] stones and arrows rained through the air, fire and blood, rubble and corpses covered Jerusalem's streets and squares. But the besieged fought like lions and met the precisely aimed power of Roman siege-craft with heroic courage.

The radical Jewish Zealots had won the people over to their slogan *Victory or death!* They prized rashness and unconditional commitment, and they despised the reasonableness of the ruling aristocrats. The revolutionaries stirred up the masses against the city's leaders, whom they called "Romanettes," and they demanded that power be handed over to "the people." Those who rejected the fanatics' daring were branded traitors. Those who suggested that the radical position would inevitably result in Jerusalem's downfall were persecuted.

Soon, in the course of the disastrous internecine conflicts erupting within the Zealot party now in control of the government, the grain reserves were set on fire.[5] In besieged Jerusalem people were starving. The audacious fighters faced doom in the form of plague, madness, and death. Exhausted by hunger, some secretly left the city. To terrorize the besieged population, Titus, the head commander of the Roman troops, ordered that these refugees be nailed to crosses facing the city wall. "The number of those crucified was so great that there was no more room for crosses, and no more crosses for bodies."[6]

Rabbi Johanan ben Zakkai, the much respected vice president of the Sanhedrin, had overlooked nothing in his learning—"not from the Bible, the Mishnah, nor the Talmud,[7] not from *halachah* or *aggadah*, not from the subtleties of the Torah and its scribes, not from astronomy or geometry, or from the conversations of the serving angels and the demons, or the murmuring of palms, or washtub tales, or animal fables."[8] He seemed to approve of what his brothers were doing in the early days of their defensive war. But when the Zealots instituted their reign of terror, he is supposed to have said to them, "All you will accomplish is that the city will be devastated and this house (the Temple) will be destroyed by fire."[9] He saw the futility of fighting against the superpower, Rome. Only peace would prevent Jerusalem's utter destruction.

To deceive the guards, Rabbi Johanan had his students lay him in a coffin and carry him out of the city as a corpse at dusk. He went to the Roman commander and asked permission to open a House of Learning in the Roman-occupied town of Yavne, near Jaffa. Permission was granted.[10]

"Forty years before the destruction of the Temple the gleaming red woolen strip did not turn white, the western lamp did not burn, and the Temple doors opened on their own, until Rabbi Johanan ben Zakkai shouted at them, 'Temple, why are you frightened (and why do you frighten us)?! I know that you will ultimately be destroyed, for the prophet (Zechariah 11:1) has already proclaimed that fire will burn your cedars.'"[11] Seized by this premonition, he is supposed to have said, alluding to the Zealots, "When the young men say to you, 'We want to construct the Temple,' do not listen to them. And when the old men say, 'We want to destroy the Temple,' listen to them. Because the young men's construction is destruction and the old people's destruction is construction."[12]

Rabbi Johanan's attitude and behavior remind us of the great prophetic figures. Like a prophet, he understood how to recognize divine providence in the maze of events. Like Jeremiah in an earlier time, at the last moment he urged mutual understanding. But—like the orgiastic suggestions of the false prophets in Jeremiah's time[13]—the national ardor of the Jewish Zealots and the messianic enthusiasts found its way into the hearts of the Jews more easily than Rabbi Johanan's austere faith. Absolute devotion was easier and more acceptable than insightful acceptance.

The Temple was in flames. As if upon its ruins there

arose a power that gave a new and firm form to the spiritual and moral essence of the people. The creator and founder of this metamorphosis was Rabbi Johanan ben Zakkai: the sanctity of the Temple was transferred to the House of Learning; the study of Torah took the place of the sacrificial offering.

At the time, mystical speculations, apocalyptic visions, and messianic exaltation ruled men's minds. Sects, secret societies, and pseudo-messianic movements were astir among the people. Rabbi Johanan, whose plea for peace in the atmosphere of battle must have made him seem passé, became the herald of intellectualism. The study of the Torah was to be the sole task of Jewish scholarship and education. Rabbi Johanan, himself an outstanding master of mysticism, sought to prevent the spread of Jewish mysticism by forbidding instruction in the secret teachings to even one single person, "unless he is a wise man and understands it based on his own knowledge."[14]

In Yavne the foundation was laid for a pyramid whose completion would remain the task and opportunity of the future. In laying this foundation, Rabbi Johanan was not only a molder of Jewish history, but comparable to, say, Ezra the Scribe: he showed how a definitive political catastrophe could be transformed into a moral and spiritual recovery.

The power that gave this new form life issued from a source that Rabbi Johanan had shared in discovering: tradition. The significance once attributed to *revelation* and its promulgation was now passed on to *tradition* and its preservation for the present and the future. According to posterity, Rabbi Johanan ben Zakkai never said anything that he had not heard from his teachers,[15] whose teachings must have been magnificent. Of the knowledge that he had received from his teachers and whose boundless dimensions he, himself, had identified, he claimed, "And, even so, from their learnedness I have taken only as much as a gull that has dipped into the ocean."[16]

For the people, the sanctuary in Jerusalem was the visual manifestation of the Beyond, an enduring miracle. Its destruction was a theft from the imagination of the believer. The destruction of the Temple was the destruction of a magnificent legend. To what concrete symbol should the energy that stemmed from devotion and wonder now turn?

Through Rabbi Johanan ben Zakkai *the myth of learnedness* came into being. From here on, teaching, knowledge, and wisdom become the themes around which the tales of the people are woven. A transformed attitude of the soul generates new ideals. A novel dream-world comes into being: Rabbi Johanan ben Zakkai is supposed to have said, "If all heaven were parchments and all trees quills and all seas ink, these would not suffice to record what I know."[17]

He showed the shaken people how this new life is lived. It is said of him that he never walked four cubits without Torah and tefillin, he never spoke in idle conversation, no one ever arrived at the House of Learning before him, he never thought about issues of Torah while walking in dirty alleyways, when he left the House of Learning he never left anyone behind, one saw him only studying, never just sitting about, and he never said that it was time to leave the House of Learning.[18]

What made him exceptional was not so much the depth of his thinking as the breadth and manifoldness of his knowledge. No new methods, no pathbreaking teachings have come down from him. He owes his place in the intellectual history of our people not to the ingenuity of his thinking but to the *humanity* of his character. "No one passing him on the street—not even a stranger—ever greeted him before being greeted by him first,"[19] and yet he said: "A person—a servant of God, after all—who takes another's yoke upon himself, is an unworthy being."[20] "Iron may not be used to construct the altar because it is used as a weapon of war."[21] "A person who creates peace between individuals, between man and wife, family and family, city and city, people and people, kingdom and kingdom will be spared God's judgment."[22] He emphasized the concern of divine Law for the dignity of the sinner, too, and liked to say, "Look, how God preserves the honor of His creatures...."[23]

Foreseeing the future, Hillel, whose youngest student was Rabbi Johanan,[24] is supposed to have called him "the father of wisdom and the father of the coming generations."[25] Scorning complacency, he, the forefather of Jewish learning, coined the adage, "Even if you have learned a great deal, don't take any credit for it, for that is what you were born to."[26]

When he became ill, his students visited him and said, "Light of Israel, its right column, its mighty hammer, why are you crying?" He answered saying, "If you brought me before a king of flesh and blood who is here today and in the grave tomorrow, I would still cry. Now, when I am being brought before the King of Kings, I shouldn't cry?" They said to him, "Master, bless us!" He answered, "May you fear God as you fear another person." His students said to him, "Only that much?" He answered, "Oh, were it only so! Take note, when a person commits a sin, he says, 'May no one be watching me!'"[27]

"With his death wisdom's glow was gone forever."[28]

Rabbi Gamliel II

Rabbi Gamliel II was the first *nasi* of the post-temple Sanhedrin. When he took office in approximately 80 CE, the stakes were high for Jewish legal arguments: after the destruction of the Temple, the sacrificial ritual led by the high priests could no longer define the center of Jewish practice and identity; instead, the decisions of the scholars in the house of study, led by the *nasi*, would set the new parameters of the Jewish way of life. Fierce disagreements ensued about the correct processes and outcomes, and it took a strong and wise leader to find a path to cohesion.

Heschel identifies the main disputants in these arguments as the Hillelites and the Shammaites. Hillel and Shammai were scholars and religious leaders in Jerusalem at the end of the first century BCE and the beginning of the first century CE. The Talmud abounds in stories about their differences, both in personal style and in approach to Jewish law. They each had disciples, and they each established academies in their names, known as the House of Hillel and the House of Shammai. Though their controversies have been described as "disputes for the sake of heaven," the lifeblood of Jewish legal discussion (see Pirkei Avot 5:20), some sources portray their confrontations as bloody. Talmud Yerushalmi (Shabbat 1.4 [3c]) describes a violent scene in the House of Learning when decisions were being made about Jewish law: "The students of the House of Shammai stood below them and they began to slaughter the students of the House of Hillel. It was taught: six of them ascended and the others stood over them with swords and lances."

In the disputes between the Houses of Hillel and Shammai, Rabbi Gamliel II leaned toward the Hillelites. Hillel was known for his personal kindness and forbearance, and his academy is described as a place where students conducted themselves with humility and great respect for the opinions of others. Shammai and his students, on the other hand, are characterized as arrogant and as silencers

43

of dissent. In fact, the Talmud cites this difference as the reason that—even though both are "words of the living God"—Hillel's rulings become the law. In his discussion of Rabbi Gamliel II, Heschel notes an irony: Gamliel's tactics in support of Hillel over Shammai seem harsh, disrespectful, even arrogant.

Twice, Heschel refers to an event that provoked a bifurcation of the Israelite nation in another era. In 1 Kings 11, Rehoboam, the son of Solomon and the grandson of David, inherits the throne of the Davidic dynasty. The people petition him, asking that he reduce their heavy taxes, a legacy of Solomon's reign. He responds, "My father imposed a heavy yoke on you, and I will add to your yoke; my father flogged you with whips, but I will flog you with scorpions" (1 Kings 12:11). As a result, the ten tribes that inhabit the northern territories revolt against Rehoboam's harsh leadership. They secede, creating two separate kingdoms—Israel in the north and Judah in the south—that will never reunite. Their division is the beginning of the end of the Davidic monarchy. Heschel credits Rabbi Gamliel II with averting a similar disaster in his own time.

This essay was first published in the *Gemeindeblatt der jüdischen Gemeinde zu Berlin* on March 8, 1936.

Jerusalem lay in ruins, and discord was tearing the people apart. The differences in the views of the Shammaites and the Hillelites had been in conflict for over a century. Before the destruction of the Temple they had led to bloody confrontations until they were temporarily stilled by war, but now these old controversies spread like creepers. The soil of Palestine, having been violently stirred up by the thunderstorms of revolt, was especially receptive to them, and there they blossomed and thrived. They struck deep into theory and practice, into the study of the law, and into people's thinking generally. Unimpeded, they sucked out all the earth's juices. There was no area of religious, social, economic, or marital life over which the contending parties had not quarreled, and they compromised on nothing. Their various intellectual passions focused on the study of the law, which was now the burning center of activity, and they sundered the unity of teaching and life. "One Torah had become two."[29]

In an earlier time one split had brought about the downfall of the ten tribes, and another the breaking away of the Karaites.[30] But at this time, when the consequences of the governmental and moral catastrophe were causing the nation to bleed from every limb and to suffer significant losses when various factions joined sects, such a loss would have been very difficult to overcome.

The nation's very core was also weakened to the breaking point by the split between the learned elite and the masses. That is to say, the so-called "people of the land" (*am ha'aretz*) were frivolously lax in their observance of the religious laws. They often refused, for example, to pay the tithe, and they also resisted the numerous precepts governing purity. The scribes, who took the exact observance of these requirements seriously, formed a group (known as *haverim*) and avoided all contact with the "people of the land." They did not eat with them, they did not touch them, they did not intermarry, they would not serve as witnesses for them, they would not designate them as guardians or as holders of charitable offices, and they would not travel in their company. This rift shook the nation's social foundations. The estrangement between the educated class and the masses, who in any case had been left shabby, disordered, and uncivilized by revolution and war, meant that "the people of the land" became completely ignorant. They became "plebs."

"People of the land cannot be pious. They are like a servant who has never learned to cook and, if he tried, would ruin the dishes."[31] The forbearing Rabbi Johanan ben Zakkai had asserted that the inhabitants of the Galilee were "enemies of the Torah."[32] They, who as a group were closed to the outside by their shared convictions (if not also by their common origin), looked down on "ordinary folk" with contempt and together formed something like a caste, which was, however, utterly torn apart by internal divisions.

Nor could the academy of Rabbi Johanan ben Zakkai assert itself as a central institution. When he died, his most important disciples, Rabbi Eliezer ben Hyrkanos and Rabbi Joshua ben Hanina, left Yavne in order to found their own houses of learning in Lydda and Pekiin.

"When the teachers in the Yavne Academy came together, they said, 'One day the Torah will be forgotten in Israel, because it is said: Days will come, says the Lord, when I will send hunger into the land—not hunger for bread, not thirst for water, but for hearing the words of the Lord. But they will not find it.'"[33] Given the mood of the time, this was understood to mean that the Torah might be forgotten.

The leader of the Jews—also recognized as such by the Roman authorities—was the patriarch Rabbi Gamliel (the Second) of the House of David. From his forefathers he inherited not only the princely dignity of the patriarchate, but also decisiveness, energy, and a talent for the confident deployment of his power. He was a superb tactician and by nature the opposite of his teacher and predecessor, Johanan ben Zakkai. Elegant and purposeful, he was characterized less by scholarliness than by strength of will and administrative ability. Seeing clearly the demands of the times and the counterforces of the opposition, he understood that only with strict rule could he master the prevailing anarchy. The innermost core of his politics was to reestablish the unity of the Teaching. But to try to exorcise the deep-seated particularism[34] from the world was a risky venture indeed.

This steely patriarch led with a powerful arm. Only centralization, the establishment of a legislative institution whose authority was widely acknowledged and respected, would save the Teaching and the nation from complete dissolution. He executed his intentions relentlessly and courageously. He succeeded in giving the decisions of the Sanhedrin—the central Jewish agency of communal administration, of which he was the head—the force of law. With unyielding discipline, he established the authority of the office of the patriarch. "No student whose opinions do not match his appearance may enter the House of Learning" was one of Rabbi Gamliel's rules, and he posted guards at the entrance.[35]

After the destruction of the Temple, when the synagogue came to replace the sacrifice, prayer acquired essential significance. Rabbi Gamliel set forth form, content and times of observance in precise detail.[36] His orders put a stop to the disarray in a liturgy that gnostic and heretical turmoil was threatening to reduce to complete confusion. The formulations of the prayers were edited, the number of benedictions fixed to eighteen (hence the appellation "Eighteen Benedictions"), and a confessional text was inserted into the prayers to mark a clear separation from the sectarians.[37] This regimentation aroused some resistance. The opponents understood prayer as a service of the heart that should therefore have no fixed form but rather be spoken out of one's own capacity. In spite of the opposition, however, the patriarch succeeded in implementing these changes.

Rabbi Gamliel, who was also well versed in astronomy, insisted that only the patriarch would have the right to establish the dates of the calendar, which until then had been based on the testimony of observers of the new moon.[38] He ruthlessly thwarted the opposition that first met this decision. When Rabbi Joshua once declared as unreliable the observers' testimony on which Rabbi Gamliel based his determination for the beginning of the month of Tishrei and proposed another date, Rabbi Gamliel said to him, "I order you to come to me with a stick and money on the day that according to your calculations will be the Day of Atonement."[39] Rabbi Joshua, facing this walk to Canossa, was very upset. Nevertheless, with stick and money in hand he went to Yavne on the day that he had calculated to be the Day of Atonement. When the patriarch saw him, he rose from his chair, kissed him on the head and said, "Peace be unto you, my teacher and student! Praise be to the age in which the great obey the small."[40]

Rabbi Gamliel's attempts to overcome the anarchy that had been unleashed by the quarrels between the parties were of greatest importance. He brought the most significant disagreements between the Hillelites and the

Shammaites before the Sanhedrin in Yavne, where they were decided by vote. Only the Sanhedrin could validate the laws. The discussions lasted three years. The question of which of the two schools was to have precedence was, according to legend, solved by a higher inspiration. Rabbi Gamliel, who was known to have experienced inspiration, may have reached for an oracle. A voice from heaven is said to have pronounced, "The teachings of both schools are words of the living God, but in practice the Hillelite principles alone are valid."[41]

At first the Shammaites refused to rely on such signs. They believed that tradition, not a new revelation, was the recognized source of the Teaching. They were also embittered by the harshness of the rebuke, the exclusivity of study in the Academy and especially the patriarch's excommunication of respected scholars.[42] The strictness was misinterpreted as hunger for power. Was it not to be feared that these harsh regulations—which, by an irony of history, were intended to legitimate the Hillelite teachings—might have an effect similar to Rehoboam's threats to punish the people with whips and scorpions?

The opponents' outrage over Rabbi Gamliel's authoritarian behavior, which was first aired by disrupting meetings of the Sanhedrin, finally broke into outright hostility. During an open meeting the patriarch accused Rabbi Joshua, with whom he also had a dispute about a case of a firstborn, of secret opposition to the Sanhedrin's decision about the evening prayer. When Rabbi Joshua denied this, the patriarch said, "Joshua, stand up, so that one can testify against you." Then Rabbi Joshua stood up and said that one could not accuse him of lying.

Rabbi Gamliel sat and held forth, while Rabbi Joshua remained standing, until the people began to murmur and called to the speaker of the patriarch:[43] Desist. Then he desisted. The people spoke: How much longer will he torment him?! Last year he tormented him about the New Year, he tormented him about the firstborn, and now he torments him again. Let's go! Let's remove him![44]

But with whom shall we replace him? If we choose Rabbi Joshua, well, it's for his sake that we deposed the patriarch in the first place. Let us choose Rabbi Eleazar ben Azaria, for he is wise, wealthy and a tenth-generation descendant of Ezra. So they came to him and said, "Would the Master agree to head the College?" He replied, "I will consult with my people at home." His wife spoke to him, "They could throw you out and bring grief upon you. As of yet, you haven't a single white hair." At that time he was eighteen years old, and a miracle occurred: eighteen rows of hair turned white.[45]

On that day the door guard was removed and the students were given permission to enter. On that day seven hundred benches were added. Then Rabbi Gamliel became discouraged and said, "Maybe, God forbid, I have kept the Torah from Israel. . . ."[46]

It seems that "on that day" the decisions that had been arrived at in Hillel's spirit during Rabbi Gamliel's time in office were subject to a thorough revision. The principles and points of view of the schools were reviewed, and probing testimony was taken on the old traditions. The collection of these testimonies has been preserved in the tractate "The Testimonies" (Eduyot).[47]

Free of resentment and true to his principle that the

decisions of the Sanhedrin were binding, Rabbi Gamliel took part in the discussions of the Teaching. He understood well the unfairness of his tactics and said to himself, "If this is how it's to be, I will go and ask Rabbi Joshua for forgiveness." When he entered his house and saw that the walls were black, he said to him, "I can see from the walls of your house that you are a smithy." Rabbi Joshua replied, "Woe be to the age in which you are the leader. You aren't familiar with the sufferings of scholars, and don't know how hard it is for them to feed themselves." Rabbi Gamliel said, "I yield to you! Forgive me!" But Rabbi Joshua paid him no attention. So Rabbi Gamliel asked of him, "Do this for the sake of my ancestors." Rabbi Joshua relented. Rabbi Gamliel was once again put in office, which he administered together with Rabbi Eleazar ben Azaria, who had been named in the interval.[48]

This conciliatory behavior reveals the polarity between tactics and character in Rabbi Gamliel's life. The energetic patriarch with the imperious manner was by nature softhearted. Once, the son of a woman in his neighborhood died, and at night she cried for him. When Rabbi Gamliel heard her voice, he cried along with her until his eyelashes fell out.[49] He taught, "Whoever feels compassion for his fellow human being will find compassion in heaven, and he who feels no compassion will find none in heaven."[50]

He enjoyed a strong friendship with his slave, Tabi. When Tabi died, Rabbi Gamliel accepted condolences and praised his virtues.[51]

In personal relationships he was forbearing, mild and modest. He suffered greatly when he thought about the impossibility of meeting the demands of true justice. And in an hour of worship, regarding an excommunication that he had imposed, he confessed, "Creator of the world! To you alone it is clear that I did this not for the sake of my honor, nor for the reputation of my house, but for the sake of your honor, so that discord does not gain the upper hand in Israel."[52]

He was wealthy, worldly and sophisticated, and he carried himself with dignity. By nature sickly, he had to travel often, even as far as Rome. Since he associated with representatives of the government, he and his relatives were granted exceptional permission to be educated in Greek and Roman, to have their hair cut in the heathen style and to use a mirror.[53]

He would sometimes say that a public office is not about ruling, but rather submission and service.[54]

He held office for several decades. When he died, he was buried like a king.[55]

"It is taught: for their relatives, the burial of the dead used to be worse than death itself (because of the great expense it incurred), so that they abandoned the corpse and ran away. Then Rabbi Gamliel came and simplified things for himself, and he was buried in linen garments (according to the instructions of his will). Following his example, it became the custom for everyone to bury their dead in linen garments."[56]

Rabbi Akiba

Rabbi Akiba was a major figure of Rabbinic lore, a teacher of Torah in the late first and early second centuries of the Common Era. He died a martyr's death at the hands of the Romans during the Bar Kochba rebellion of 132 to 135 CE—the rebellion on which he had placed almost messianic hopes. According to the Talmud (Bavli Berachot 61b), he was gruesomely executed for continuing to teach Torah in public in blatant disregard of Roman policy.

Heschel presents Rabbi Akiba as a creative force in establishing the validity of the Oral Law. Rabbi Akiba's interpretive methods were intended to show that each element of the Oral Law had a basis in the Written Law, even if its secrets were hidden to all but the most imaginative reader.

The essay begins with a talmudic tale that collapses the ages between Moses—receiver of the Written Law—and Rabbi Akiba—supporter of the Oral Law. The setting is a Rabbinic classroom where Rabbi Akiba is the teacher. According to custom, advanced students would sit in the first rows, so it is significant that in this vignette Moses is seated near the back of the classroom. This story appears in the Talmud in the context of a discussion of the proper calligraphy for writing the letters of a Torah scroll. In the scribal tradition, many of the letters are written with little "crowns." For example, in the Torah scroll, the letters *gimmel* and *shin* might be written as in figure 2.

The story implies that God himself affixed these crowns in order to provide interpretive material for Rabbi Akiba. Like other peculiarities in the biblical text, they were designed as hooks to which Rabbi Akiba would eventually tie the orally received traditions, securing their connection with the revealed Written Law.

Fig. 2.

This essay was first published in the *Gemeindeblatt der jüdischen Gemeinde zu Berlin* on March 29, 1936.

"When Moses ascended to heaven, he met the Holy One, blessed be He, who was attaching crowns to the letters of the Torah. Moses said to Him, 'Master of the Universe, what is this for?' He answered, 'A man who will live many generations hence named Akiba ben Joseph will one day give teaching upon teaching based on every point of the crowns.' Then Moses said to Him, 'Master of the Universe, show him to me.' He replied, 'Turn around.' Moses turned around and sat down behind the eighth row [of Akiba's students]. He didn't understand what they were discussing, which dismayed him greatly. But when Akiba gave a ruling and his students asked him how he had come to it, and he said that it was a teaching that had been revealed to Moses at Sinai, Moses was relieved. Thereupon Moses turned around, stood before the Holy One, blessed be He, and said, 'Master of the Universe, you have such a man and yet you give the Torah through me!' He answered, 'Silence! This is my will.' Thereupon he said to Him, 'Master of the Universe, you have shown me his wisdom, now show me also his reward.' He said, 'Turn around.' Moses turned around and saw Akiba's martyred body. Then Moses said to Him, 'Master of the Universe, that is the Torah, and this is its reward?' He responded, 'Silence! This is my will.'"[57]

The imagination is capable of no greater homage than this myth, according to which Rabbi Akiba surpassed Moses, who held him to be worthier than himself. Such an evaluation—accorded by the Jews to no one other than

Rabbi Akiba—was not idle praise. Rabbi Akiba's role in Oral Law can indeed be compared to Moses's role in Written Law. Rabbi Akiba's words had the impact of revelations whose scope was greater than Moses's. "Many laws that were unknown to Moses were revealed to Rabbi Akiba."[58]

Except for the de facto recognition accorded by actual practice, the validity of the immense and varied abundance of principles that Rabbi Akiba had uncovered as Oral Law was only theoretical. Their authority was seriously threatened—externally by the attacks of those who rejected "Oral Teaching" and internally by the irreconcilable controversies of the sages, but above all by a hardly justifiable sense of opposition between Written and Oral Teaching. The majority decisions of the Sanhedrin could lend the shine of a prestige conferred extrinsically, by official authority; the laws gained an authority that did not originate from the laws themselves. In an age of total insecurity this solution, seeking to prop the Teaching on an institutional base, must have seemed very questionable.

The assumption that the Oral Teaching is inherent in the Bible was Rabbi Akiba's seminal thought. Through the virtuosic artistry of his interpretations he was able to discover the one inside the other. To a certain degree he altered the very texture of the Bible: the frozen words began to thaw, to flow, and alongside the explicit readings, unsuspected meanings and intuited traditions bubbled forth.

He had a new relationship to the Bible. He sensed that its words are containers for undivulged teachings, that the Torah is full of signs and hints. His goal was to fathom these signs and to interpret them, revealing new layers of the Bible. The astonishing dimensions

55

that were exposed by this powerful expansion excited the attention of his contemporaries.

The principle of Akiba's interpretative method was that the linguistic character of the Torah is entirely different from that of human writing. The latter uses forms of expression that are either superfluous to an understanding of the text or, at the least, do not contribute directly to its content. In the language of Torah, however, nothing is *form*. Everything is *essential*, everything is *content*. Even grammatical elements, stylistic idioms, rhetorical embellishments, peculiarities of expression, even orthographic irregularities, particles and the most unprepossessing parts of the sentence point to a meaning. In this way every word became the basis for a transmitted or newly derived meaning.

Rabbi Akiba not only uncovered the congruence between Bible and Tradition; he was also the first person to systematize the Oral Tradition. The enormous body of transmitted material had been completely unorganized, the endless mass of principles and rulings, customs, and decisions having been passed down chaotically from generation to generation.

Rabbi Akiba created the first outlines of a system, and from the fragmentary and jumbled pieces he built a single pedagogical structure, the so-called Mishnah of Rabbi Akiba,[59] from which would later emerge the Mishnah edited by Rabbi Judah. "If Rabbi Akiba had not stood up in his time, the Torah would have been forgotten in Israel."[60]

"Once, when the elders were gathered in the upper story of Nitsa's house in Lydda,[61] the question was raised whether study or action was more important. Rabbi Tarfon thought action was more important. Then Rabbi Akiba spoke, saying study is more important. Thereupon all agreed with him."[62] The decision for the primacy of theory had the strongest influence not only on the Jewish way of life, but also especially on the development of their thinking. It cultivated an "intellectual narcissism," a self-sufficiency of theory, and in this way determined a very far-reaching style of thinking whose posing of problems was unconcerned with practical meaning and applicability and usefulness. Rabbi Akiba can be regarded as the forefather of *pilpul*.[63]

Jewry found itself in a time of cultural change. The Temple, the state, the aristocracy, the parties had been destroyed. The cultic and political powers, the religious, mystical, poetic, and scholarly energies dissolved almost entirely into the generating of a new fruit: the Talmud.[64] Engagement with the Talmud became the living manifestation of the people, traditional scholarship became a holy activity, education the highest value. In the place of priests and politicians, whose role had been played out, scholars stepped in—a highly significant sociological fact.

This enormous change had started before Rabbi Akiba. It was apparently due to his efforts that this new movement could flow into the hearts of the entire people. It gained thousands of disciples and thereby forged countless channels through which the current could stream into all circles of Jewry.

Engagement with the Talmud became the central idea. In the age of the Maccabees it was the sanctification of the Sabbath or circumcision for whose sake the Jews suffered a martyr's death. Now it was the study of the Talmud for which they were ready to devote and give their lives. The Talmud was the element in which people lived, the air they breathed, the basic condition for national existence.

"The Romans once decreed that the Jews were not allowed to engage with the Torah. Then Papos ben Jehuda came along and met Rabbi Akiba, who held open gatherings and read Torah. He said to him, 'Akiba, aren't you afraid of the Romans' power?' Rabbi Akiba replied, 'I will tell you a parable. A fox once went along the shore of a river, and when he saw fish fleeing from place to place he said to them: What are you afraid of? They answered: Of the nets that the people cast for us. Then he said to them: So you might want to come onto the land, and we will live together as my ancestors once did with your ancestors. Whereupon the fishes answered: Are you really the one they call the cleverest of all animals? You aren't clever, but stupid. If we are afraid in the place of our life, how much more would we be afraid in the place of our death! So it is with us. If it is like this when we engage with the Torah, of which it is said: for thereby you shall have life and shall long endure (Deuteronomy 30:20), how much more so, when we turn from it!' It is said that after several days, Rabbi Akiba was arrested and imprisoned."[65]

The man who bore this martyr's suffering was of a passionate and sensual nature. He had an eye for the beauty of landscape, colors, and the human body. His life and thought were filled with a mystical romanticism.

Until his fortieth year, Rabbi Akiba, who descended

from a line of proselytes, was a shepherd of the wealthy Ben Kalba Sabua. "When Ben Kalba Sabua's daughter saw how chaste and honest he was, she said to him, 'Will you go away to the Academy if I agree to be married to you?' He said, 'Yes.' She was then secretly married to him, and he went to the Academy. When Ben Kalba Sabua learned this, he banished her from his house and disinherited her. Rabbi Akiba remained at the Academy for twelve years, and when he returned he brought 12,000 students with him. Behind his house he heard someone saying to his wife, who lived in great poverty, 'Your father did the right thing with you. First, Akiba isn't your equal, and second, while still alive he left you a widow.' But she replied, 'If he listened to me, he could stay away another twelve years.' Then Rabbi Akiba said, 'Since she permits it, I will turn around.' Whereupon he remained at the Academy another twelve years and returned with 24,000 students. As the entire town was going to greet him, she stood up to greet him, too. When she came up to him, she fell to the ground, prostrated herself and kissed his feet. His students pushed her back, but he said, 'Leave her alone. What is mine and yours is hers.'"[66]

Even in his lifetime his reputation reached "from one end of the world to the other."[67] His contemporary Rabbi Tarfon said to him, "He who separates from you, separates from life."[68] Rabbi Akiba, who held no official position, enjoyed the same unquestioned authority in learned circles as with the people. Nevertheless, he said, "There are many Akibas in the street."[69]

He collected and administered the funds for the poor.[70] He commanded his son, "It is better to treat the Sabbath as a weekday than to leave fellow humans in need."[71] His gentleness, helpfulness, and even temper were famous. He called the biblical verse, Love your fellow as yourself (Leviticus 19:18), the main rule of the Torah. [72] Together with Rabbi Tarfon he declared, "If we had been in the Sanhedrin (when it could still apply the death penalty), no one would have ever been executed."[73]

He brought together analytic acuity with systematic farsightedness, methodic virtuosity with ingenious originality, learnedness with profundity, productivity in theory with pedagogical effectiveness, a powerful mind with a holy way of life. His personal influence was incomparable. No other master was able to gather around him such throngs of disciples.

This zealous life took a tragic turn when Rabbi Akiba applied his mystical way of life to a political game. He participated as spokesman for a delegation that was sent to Rome and, charged with official responsibilities, traveled to Babylonia. "When Bar Kochba appeared, Rabbi Akiba applied to him the biblical verse: A star will arise from Jacob."[74] He joined the revolt with messianic fervor and, seemingly, undertook further journeys to win over the masses for Bar Kochba. After the revolt collapsed, he became a victim of Roman revenge.

"The hour when Rabbi Akiba was led to his execution was just as the *Shema* was being read, and they tore his flesh with iron combs. But he accepted the yoke of the heavenly decree. His students said to him, 'Master, even now?' He replied, 'My entire life long I was troubled by the biblical verse: with all your soul (Deuteronomy 6:5)[75]—even when He takes your soul—and I thought:

When I am offered the opportunity, I will fulfill it, and now, when it is offered to me, how should I not fulfill it?' He prolonged the word *one* until his soul left on that word. Then a voice from heaven sounded, 'Joy to you, Rabbi Akiba, that your soul departed on the word *one!*' The ministering angels said in the presence of the Holy One, blessed be He, 'Is that the Torah and is that its reward?' He replied to them, 'His portion is in the future life.' Thereupon a voice sounded from heaven and said, 'Joy to you, Rabbi Akiba, you are destined for the life of the world to come.'"[76]

Rabbi Shimon ben Gamliel II

Rabbi Shimon ben Gamliel II, as his name suggests, was the son of Rabbi Gamliel II, the subject of the second "Personalities" essay. Like his father, Rabbi Shimon was appointed *nasi* of a reconstituted Sanhedrin following a failed Jewish rebellion against Rome. He took office in 142 CE, a few years after the decisive failure of the Bar Kochba rebellion, leading a Sanhedrin that had relocated to the Galilean town of Usha.

Heschel presents two ways in which Rabbi Shimon ben Gamliel's leadership brought stability to the Palestinian Jewish community. First, after the destruction of the Second Temple, much of the intellectual marrow of the Jewish community had become embedded in the exhilic culture of Babylonia, just as it had after the destruction of the First Temple. By bringing home such important functions as determining the calendar, Rabbi Shimon succeeded in revitalizing Palestine as the heart of the Jewish world. Second, Rabbi Shimon helped to slant the legal and spiritual path away from the extremism and otherworldliness that characterized much of the Jewish community (as discussed in Heschel's Rabbi Akiba essay) toward a more pragmatic and accessible approach.

Heschel mentions parenthetically that Rabbi Shimon's position— that the Torah speaks in a language easily understood by the human intellect, not in a language of esoteric hints—is also the position held by Rabbi Ishmael. In Rabbinic literature, Rabbi Akiba and Rabbi Ishmael represent thesis and antithesis, two sides of a coin, much like the figures of Hillel and Shammai from an earlier era. The theological distinction associated with Rabbi Ishmael and Rabbi Akiba —between the intellectual and the emotional, the practical and the esoteric—would engage Heschel for many years. Two decades after the publication of these essays, Heschel would write his monumental study of Rabbinic thought, currently available in English translation under the title *Heavenly Torah as Refracted through the Generations*—a study of the legacy of the debates between Rabbi Akiba and Rabbi

Ishmael. The contrasts he highlights between Rabbi Akiba and Rabbi Shimon ben Gamliel in this essay foreshadow that seminal study.

This essay was first published in the *Gemeindeblatt der jüdischen Gemeinde zu Berlin* on April 12, 1936.

The position of the Holy Land in the Jewish world, that is, the relationship of the diaspora to Palestinian Jewry, had reached a crisis. After the fall of Jerusalem many Jews had settled in Syria, Asia Minor, Egypt, North Africa, and especially in Babylonia. They had come there as refugees, as prisoners of war, or as slaves. But the dream of an imminent restoration of the Temple and of the authority of the Sanhedrin (working out of Yavne) ensured the survival of Palestine's spiritual hegemony.

After the collapse of the Bar Kochba revolt, the country was completely decimated, not only economically but also spiritually. Jerusalem was transformed into a heathen city and renamed Aelia Capitolina, where the Jews were forbidden entrance upon pain of death. Emperor Hadrian's repressive measures, especially the prohibitions against Torah study, circumcision, and rest on the seventh day, were intended to destroy the nation spiritually. Roman enforcers roamed through the country, and anyone who held to the customs of their fathers had to be prepared to die. People who were especially hard hit by the Hadrianic measures, among them teachers of the law, began to emigrate in large numbers. Spiritual life in Palestine ceased. The House of Learning in Yavne shut down.

About the emigration of the scholars it is told: "When they left the country, they all wept, tore their clothes and said, 'Living in Palestine offsets the requirement to fulfill all the Torah's laws . . . .'"[77]

One of these scholars, Hanania, settled in the city of Nehar Pekod in Babylonia. There he founded a House of Learning and set up a court tribunal to determine the calendar[78]—a responsibility the Palestinian Sanhedrin could no longer fulfill because of the Hadrianic persecutions. With this, Palestine—where hardly any well-known scholars now remained—lost its prerogatives.

Over time, however, the Roman view of the Jews was to change. In Rome one night, some holy teachers of the law passed by the rulers' houses and called, "By heaven, are we not your brothers, are we not the children of one father, are we not the children of one mother? In what way are we different from all the other peoples and tribes, that you persecute us so mercilessly?"[79]

The lifting of the Hadrianic edicts, which according to the talmudic tale was brought about by this procession, made it possible for the Jews to slowly rebuild the framework for their self-governance in Palestine.[80] The teachers, among them some who had returned from Babylonia, came together in Usha, a Galilean town, and discussed the restoration of Jewish communal life. The Sanhedrin was founded anew and Rabbi Shimon, son of Rabbi Gamliel II, was elected patriarch.

In his father's house the young dignitary had received an education not only in Jewish but also in Greek wisdom,[81] and he took an interest in physiology and botany.[82] His energy and political talents, which he had inherited from his father, enabled him to carry out the restoration of Palestinian Jewry.

The patriarch sent a group of emissaries to Nehar Pekod. They said to Hanania: "The kids that you left behind have grown into horned billy goats. They sent us to you with the words: Go and speak to him in our name (saying, given the restoration in Palestine, that he should dissolve the Sanhedrin in Babylonia). If he obeys, all is well. If not, a ban will be pronounced over him. And tell this to our brothers in the diaspora. If they obey, all is well. If not, they should go up on a mountain and erect an altar, Hanania should play on the harp and everyone together should deny God and say, 'The God of Israel is not ours!'" Whereupon the entire people began to cry loudly, "Heaven forbid! The God of Israel is ours!" (Why all this? Because it is said: Torah emanates from Zion and the word of the Lord from Jerusalem—Isaiah 2:3.)[83] The authority of the Palestinian Sanhedrin had been reinstated.

It was necessary, however, to renew not only institutions, but also spiritual life. The collapse of the revolt had not resulted in a collapse of faith but rather in an avalanche of resignation, and it went through the Jewish nation with disastrous effects. Enthusiastic faith was sublimated into contempt for the world, valor into despairing rage. The Jews were forfeiting their relationship to reality.

Rabbi Shimon ben Gamliel came to be in profound intellectual opposition to Rabbi Akiba. Rabbi Akiba had taught, "Learning is higher than doing,"[84] whereas Rabbi Shimon ben Gamliel insisted, "Not the teaching but the doing is the main thing."[85] Rabbi Akiba saw an object of interpretation in every turn of phrase of the Torah.[86] Rabbi Shimon ben Gamliel, on the other hand (like Rabbi

Ishmael), was of the opinion that the Torah employed a hyperbolic manner of speech that one needn't take literally.[87] Rabbi Akiba and his school valued dialectical analysis over the acquisition of mere knowledge, whereas Rabbi Shimon ben Gamliel valued knowledge over intellectual acuity.

This opposition was made even more obvious when Rabbi Akiba's students, who were Rabbi Shimon ben Gamliel's contemporaries, took their master's principles to extremes. The priority given to learning had originally been based on the justification, "Learning leads to action."[88] For Rabbi Akiba's students, learning had been a priority that wasn't merely privileged but exclusive: Rabbi Shimon ben Yochai[89] said, "If we plow when it's time to plow, sow when it's time to sow, cut when it's time to cut, thresh when it's time to thresh, and mill when the wind is blowing, what will then become of the Torah?"[90]

Rabbi Shimon ben Yochai withdrew with his son to a cave. When they emerged after twelve years and saw the people plowing and sowing, Rabbi Shimon said, "They are neglecting eternal life and busying themselves with temporal life." According to legend, every place to which they directed their eyes immediately went up in flames. Then a voice sounded from heaven, "Have you emerged only to destroy my world? Return to your cave."[91]

When the Romans forbade engagement with the Teaching, a movement arose among the Jews to avoid marriage, since they didn't want to bear children who couldn't receive instruction in the Torah.[92]

The urge to exhaust the Torah's mysterious wealth of meaning that had inspired Rabbi Akiba's school resulted in an increase of idealistically exaggerated ethical and ritual restrictions. The sin of "intellectual narcissism" became evident in the school of Rabbi Meir, who was Rabbi Akiba's student. Indifference to the realities of life degenerated into arrogance.

At a meeting of the teachers in the upper story of Nitsa's house in Lydda,[93] it was decided that a Jew was obliged to forfeit his life only in the three following situations: when forced to commit idolatry, a sexual offense, or murder.[94] Rabbi Akiba, on the other hand, who taught the love of suffering and longed all his life to sacrifice his soul for God, never desisted from Torah study, even though it meant risking death.[95] He became the source for a boundless willingness to submit to martyrdom, which at that time could have seriously imperiled the survival of the Jewish people.

Rabbi Shimon ben Gamliel, realistic and thoughtful, championed the primary value of life and opposed those ideologies that ignored reality. On the question of marriage, he thought that one must not let Israel perish. The principle of "the preservation of the world" was the governing thought behind his legislation. One is permitted to desecrate the Sabbath for the sake of a one-day-old child, "for the Torah says that *one* Sabbath may be desecrated for his sake in order that he may keep many Sabbaths."[96] His basic principle was that a burdensome rule could be imposed on the community only when a majority could bear it. "Every commandment that the Jews have received with joy is fulfilled by them with joy. What they have received without joy, they fulfill without joy."[97]

The primacy of practical considerations determined his entire life. He had set no scholarly goals for himself, and his energies were directed mainly to the legal structure of the Jewish present. The numerous rules he instituted show a preference for concrete decisions, in which he often demonstrated a special concern for women and slaves.[98] The other schools, in contrast, tended to adjudicate abstract cases that were irrelevant and, indeed, hardly applicable to contemporary life.

Some of his contemporaries were more learned than he. His character was distinguished by his prudence and levelheadedness, his understanding of life's meaning, and his determination. His critical, realistic, and independent way of thinking may be considered exemplary. By developing the theoretical basis for giving priority to knowledge over intellectual brilliance, he prepared the way for the great achievement of his son, who was to construct the system of the Mishnah.

Elisha ben Abuyah

Elisha ben Abuyah's biography is fragmentary in the Talmud, but we can assume that he was a younger contemporary of Rabbi Akiba, who had met the suffering of those times with messianic mysticism, and eventually martyrdom. Rabbi Shimon ben Gamliel, on the other hand, had responded from the perspective of humanism and pragmatism. For Elisha ben Abuyah, the suffering he saw around him led him to theological despair and apostasy.

Rabbinic literature frequently refers to Elisha ben Abuyah as Aher, Hebrew for "other." According to a story in Talmud Bavli Hagigah 15a, he acquired this nickname from a prostitute. Having lost his faith in the world to come and determined to enjoy this world, he solicits her services. Shocked that a Torah scholar would do such a thing, she says, "Aren't you Elisha ben Abuyah?!" He then picks a radish on the Sabbath (when harvesting is forbidden) and hands it to her. She responds, "He is *aher* [other]." On first reading, it seems that she calls him this because she thinks she has mistaken him for someone else. But the name sticks because for the Rabbis he plays the role of the "other"—the outsider, the non-Jew—who is, at the same time, one of "us."

Elisha ben Abuyah's intellectual leanings are subject to scholarly debate. The *Jewish Encyclopedia* reports that "according to Grätz, he was a Karpotian Gnostic; according to Siegfried, a follower of Philo; according to Dubsch, a Christian." Heschel identifies his thought with that of Philo, whose explanation of the existence of evil in a godly world included the idea that God does not act directly in creation, but delegates to a mediating power that acts on its own.

Both the Talmud and Heschel use the story of Elisha ben Abuyah as a vehicle for acknowledging and confronting the theological problem of evil. Elisha lost faith in God's power or God's will to overcome evil. After the failed Bar Kochba rebellion, with many committed Jewish leaders dying as martyrs, his apostasy must have been a terrible blow to communal morale.

This essay was first published in the *Gemeindeblatt der jüdischen Gemeinde zu Berlin* on April 26, 1936.

Elisha ben Abuyah "was sitting at his studies in the Valley of Ginosar.[99] He saw a man climb a date palm, take a mother bird from her young and climb safely back down. The next morning, he saw another man climb a date palm, take the baby birds and free the mother bird. As he was climbing down, a snake bit him, and he died. And Elisha ben Abuyah said, 'It is written: Let the mother go, and take only the young, in order that you may fare well and have a lengthened life (Deuteronomy 22:6–7).[100] In what way did he fare well? Where his lengthened life?'"[101]

Elisha ben Abuyah "saw the tongue of Rabbi Judah the Baker, in the blood-soaked maw of a dog. He said, 'Is that the Torah, and is this its reward? That is the tongue that brought forth the words of the Torah. That is the tongue that strove for Torah every day. Is that the Torah, and is this its reward? It would appear that there is no reward and no resurrection of the dead.'"[102]

To have one's faith shaken like this is nothing new in Judaism. Job is the classic case of this experience. The acceptance of a personal divinity led people to expect that their piety would be rewarded. The absence of a reward awakened tortured doubts about the truth of their faith.

Aher—as the apostate Elisha ben Abuyah was later called—had been a well-respected teacher of law, and his sense of resignation was a blow to the religious enthusiasm of the martyrs and to the spiritual aftermath of the national catastrophe. Hadrian's persecution of the Jews was directed against fulfilling the Torah. It was an attack not only on people but on God's word. It struck sinners the least and pious men the most. The apostates, on the other hand, were as if immune to the disaster. Could it be assumed that God himself wanted to spite his word?

It is apparent that Elisha ben Abuyah sought to solve the problem of theodicy through theosophical speculation. He seemed to be directing his attention to the thought that we first encounter in Philo of Alexandria, namely, that there is no direct relationship between God and the world, that God's effects on the world are mediated by intermediate beings. This attempt at a solution succeeded in evading the question, which was now no longer directed exclusively at the highest being but against the order he had established. Of this in-between entity a later tale claimed that "it brings the souls of the just to God in order to atone for Israel in the days of the Exile."[103] Even in Aher's time this idea may already have been a familiar interpretation of martyrdom. In any case, the teaching of the "in-between entity" was not only a false solution but virtually a heretical trap.

This teaching got Aher to thinking, "Maybe there are two powers in heaven?"[104] In his mind, the world and the Torah, God and Evil, stood in contrast. He couldn't find his way back to a unity, and assumed on the basis of his personal experience that they were in conflict. The fissure in his experience now seemed to him a fissure in the substance of the universe.

When this important teacher of Torah had succumbed to heresy, "a voice sounded from heaven: Turn back and repent, you apostate sons, except for Aher!"[105] Aher was damned. The call to repentance, which was directed to all people, excluded him.

"And Aher said, 'If I am expelled from that world, then I will enjoy this world.'"[106]

Aher came from a circle that included Rabbi Akiba, Ben Azzai, and Ben Zoma. They, too, had speculated about the in-between entity, presumably for reasons similar to Aher's. But they were spared both entanglement in dualism and resignation over the discrepancy between action and reward. Perhaps with a view to Aher, Ben Azzai said, "The reward for law is law, the reward for sin is sin."[107]

But Aher was receptive neither to this thought nor to the understanding of suffering as "chastisements of love,"[108] which, according to Jewish understanding, could be meted out to the pious as a test or as purification. He apparently had little sense of an inner richness, he needed external reward, and it is telling that, when he learned that he had been damned, he decided to give himself to pleasure and sensual enjoyment.

The sages kept a careful eye out for the purity of their monotheistic belief. The people—living in a world unsettled by spiritual ferment and ideological movements—could easily succumb to the onslaught of false doctrine. In this Hellenistic period the tendency to meld different religions increased the danger that elements of foreign beliefs would intrude. The period was swarming with men who founded sects and communities by adding alien beliefs to an existing religion. Jewish leaders wanted to protect Israel from this syncretism, which was a part of the interaction between the Orient and Hellas, between Eastern myth and Greek speculation.

Aher seems to have taken a stance in opposition to Rabbi Akiba. His saying, "Learning in youth is like writing with ink on new paper. But if you learn in old age, it is like writing with ink on smeared paper,"[109] could have been an allusion to Rabbi Akiba's biography.[110]

The sages, especially Rabbi Akiba, had forbidden any involvement with Greek culture.[111] But Aher carried "many heretical books with him"[112] and "Greek song was always on his lips."[113] In the spirit of his master Rabbi Akiba, Rabbi Meir explained, "Limit your activity and concern yourself with Torah. I desist from all worldly activity and teach my son only Torah."[114] When Aher went into the House of Learning and saw boys sitting before the books, he said, "Why are they sitting here? What are they doing? This one would be a mason, that one would be a carpenter, this one a fisherman, and that one a tailor. And when they heard this, they stopped what they were doing and left."[115]

The apostate became an enemy. The sages avoided any contact with Aher, now excluded and outlawed, despite his apparently outstanding erudition. Rabbi Meir was the only one who, in spite of everything, continued to associate with him.

"Once on Shabbat, Aher was riding on a horse, while Rabbi Meir followed after him in order to learn Torah from his mouth. He said to him, 'Meir, turn back, because from my horse's steps I can tell that the Sabbath zone reaches only to here.' (On the Sabbath one may go no more than two thousand cubits from the town border.)

And Rabbi Meir said to Aher, 'You, too, should turn back.' Then Aher said, 'Have I not already said to you that I have heard from behind heaven's curtain: Turn back and repent, you apostate sons, except for Aher!'"[116]

"After some time, Elisha fell ill. People came to Rabbi Meir and said to him, 'Look, your master is ill.' He went to see him, found him ill and said to him, 'Do you not wish to repent?' Elisha replied, 'And if I were to repent, would they accept it?' Then Rabbi Meir said, 'Is it not written: You allow people to repent until crushed (Psalm 90:3)[117]—until the crushing of the soul! And then they are accepted.'

"In the course of this hour Elisha wept, breathed his last and died.

"Then Rabbi Meir was happy in his heart and said, 'It seems that the master breathed his last in the midst of his repenting.'"[118]

Rabbi Meir

This essay is set in the period from 142 to 165 CE, when Rabbi Shimon ben Gamliel II was *nasi*. Rabbi Meir was a student of Elisha ben Abuyah. Although he did not follow Elisha down the path of apostasy, neither did he denounce his teacher. Throughout Mishnah, Talmud, and midrash, some statements are quoted in the names of individual Rabbis, some are identified as the words of "the sages," and some are simply prefaced with "some say" or "others say." Heschel mentions a tradition that statements attributed to "others" are actually the words of Rabbi Meir, and that his name has been excised because of his support for Elisha ben Abuyah. This conceit has the effect of extending the "otherness" of his teacher, also known as Aher (Hebrew for "other"), to Rabbi Meir himself.

Rabbi Meir was also a disciple of Rabbi Akiba, and presumably his agreement with this teacher's positions earned him the ire of Rabbi Shimon ben Gamliel described in this essay. He shared with Rabbi Akiba a penchant for complex and esoteric interpretations— what some might criticize as intellectual gamesmanship—and he elevated the value of study to mystical significance. As a corollary, he believed that the importance of the laws derived through the process of Rabbinic argumentation was equal to—or even greater than—that of explicit biblical laws.

The name "Meir," from the Hebrew root א.ו.ר—light, can be translated as "one who illuminates."

This essay was first published in the *Gemeindeblatt der jüdischen Gemeinde zu Berlin* on May 17, 1936.

"He who concerns himself with the Torah for its own sake is granted much. Moreover, he is worthy of having the whole world exist for his sake alone. He is called friend and darling, he loves God and he loves people, he delights God and he delights people. The Torah graces him with

PERSÖNLICHKEITEN DER JÜDISCHEN GESCHICHTE

Rabbi Meir
von Dr. Abraham Heschel

„Wer sich mit der Tora um ihrer selbst willen befaßt, dem sind viele Dinge beschieden; und noch mehr, er ist würdig, daß die ganze Welt nur seinetwegen bestehe. Er heißt Freund und Liebling, er liebt Gott und liebt die Menschen, er erfreut Gott und erfreut die Menschen. Die Tora bekleidet ihn mit Sanftmut und Gottesfurcht und befähigt ihn, gerecht, fromm, rechtschaffen und treu zu sein ... Sie gewährt ihm Tugend und Königtum, Herrschaft und Erforschung des Rechtes. Man offenbart ihm Geheimnisse der Tora. Er wird wie eine nie versiegende Quelle und wie ein fortwährend wachsender Strom. Er sei bescheiden, langmütig und nachsichtig."

Diese Worte, die aus einer Tiefe des Bewußtseins strömen, sind der Ausdruck geistigen Machtgefühls. Sie muten bei Rabbi Meir, „dem Leuchtenden", „der die Augen der Weisen in der Halacha aufleuchten ließ", wie Sätze der Erfahrung und der begrenzten Tatsächlichkeit an. „Die Weisen haben ihren Worten die gleiche Kraft verliehen wie den Worten der Tora", lehrte er. Soweit noch als die Behauptung von der Majestät des Gelehrten und des Katharsis, ja der heiligen Wirkung der Tora, berührt uns hier das Bewußtsein von der Magie des Geistes, von der Gnadenfülle des Gesetzesstudiums.

Rabbi Meir war einer der wirkungsreichsten Weiterbildner der überlieferten Lehre und hat durch Schlagkraft der Methode und Stärke der Phantasie dem Fortgang der talmudischen Wissenschaft folgenreichen Antrieb gegeben. Als Systematiker des Überlieferungsstoffes hat er die später erfolgte Redaktion der Mischna erst ermöglicht.

In jungen Jahren kommt er in das Lehrhaus Rabbi Akibas. Da er noch zu wenig Wissen hat, um den scharfsinnigen Vorträgen Rabbi Akibas zu folgen, geht er zu Rabbi Ischmael, bei dem er sich Wissen aneignet, und kehrt später zu Rabbi Akiba zurück, dessen Erläuterungen er nun versteht, und von dem er auch die Ordination erhält. Er wandert von Lehrer zu Lehrer und lernt die verschiedenen Schulen und Lehrweisen kennen.

Daneben übt er das Schreiberhandwerk aus. Es schreibt „schön und vortrefflich"; die Tinte, die er verwendet, ist durch eine bei den Juden zuerst von ihm eingeführte chemische Benarbung besonders dauerhaft und glänzend. Die Torarollen aus seiner Feder werden sehr gesucht, und es wird als „Weiser und Schreiber" gerühmt. Von den drei Schekalim, die ihm sein Beruf wöchentlich einträgt, wendet er ein Drittel auf Ernährung, ein Drittel auf Bekleidung und ein Drittel spendet er für arme Gelehrte. „Rabbi, was sollen deine Kinder anfangen, wenn du den Erwerb des Schreibens den Armen hingibst?" fragen ihn die Schüler. „Werden sie tugendhaft sein", erwidert er, „so wird sich an ihnen das Psalmwort erfüllen: Nicht sah ich einen Frommen verlassen. Werden sie es nicht sein, warum soll ich meinen Vermögen auf Feinde Gottes vererben?"

Geliebt und geachtet war seine berühmte Frau Beruria, die Tochter des Märtyrers Rabbi Chanina ben Teradjon. Einst als Rabbi Meir an einem Sabbatnachmittag im Lehrhaus weilte, starben seine beiden Söhne. Die Mutter trug sie ins Nebengemach und verhüllte sie mit einer Decke. Nach Sonnenuntergang kehrte Rabbi Meir heim und fragte nach den Söhnen. „Sie sind ins Lehrhaus gegangen", entgegnete Beruria. „Ich habe vergebens nach ihnen ausgeschaut", meinte Rabbi Meir. Beruria reichte ihm den Weinbecher, und er sprach den Segen des Sabbatausgangs. Wieder forschte er nach den Söhnen. „Sie sind ausgegangen und werden bald kommen", beruhigte ihn Beruria und setzte ihm Speise und Trank vor. Nach der Mahlzeit begann sie: „Rabbi, eine Frage: Vor längerer Zeit vertraute mir jemand ein kostbares Gut, und heute hat er es zurückgefordert; soll ich es ihm geben?" Entrüstet erwiderte Rabbi Meir: „Wie, ein anvertrautes Pfand willst du dich weigern, seinem Herrn zurückzugeben?" „Nur mit deiner Einwilligung", versetzte Beruria, faßte ihn bei der Hand, führte ihn zum Lager und zog die Decke hinweg. Entsetzt ich Rabbi Meir die Leichen seiner beiden Söhne und begann weinend zu rufen: „Meine Söhne, meine Lehrer, ihr habt mich mit euerer Weisheit erleuchtet." Er jammerte und

klagte. „Wie?" sprach zu ihm Beruria: „Hast du nicht gesagt, es sei Pflicht, das anvertraute Pfand dem Herrn ohne Murren zurückzugeben? Gott hat es uns gegeben, Gott hat es uns genommen, und seinen Namen wollen wir preisen."

Früh erreichte Rabbi Meir hohes Ansehen, aber auch viel Gegnerschaft. Er ist als Vortragsredner beliebt, als Fabeldichter berühmt. Das Spielerische in seinem Charakter kommt nicht nur in den 300 von ihm gedichteten Fuchsfabeln zum Ausdruck: In der Gesetzeswissenschaft wirkt der Einsatz seiner dialektischen Phantasie wie eine geistige Suggestion, und wenn es, nötig ist, kann er als römischer Ritter verkleidet auftreten. Selbstbewußt, erregbar und vielleicht mutwillig machte er zuweilen den Widerspruch der besonnenen und bedächtigen Zeitgenossen hervorrufen. Er lesnt „Tora aus dem Munde Aschers", des von allen verdammten Abtrünnigen. Als die Flammen aus dem Grabe Aschers hervorbrachen und er sie mit seinem Mantel löschte, fragten ihn seine Freunde: „Wenn du im Jenseits wärest, wen würdest du eher besuchen: deinen Vater oder deinen Lehrer? Er erwiderte: Erst meinen Vater und dann meinen Lehrer."

Die Hadrianischen Verfolgungen wirkten sich auch im persönlichen Leben Rabbi Meirs aus. Aber die Zeit, in der nun — wie er erzählte — das Schma leise, die Megilla bei Nacht und die Tora am Sabbat auf den Dächern lesen mußte, da der Späher lauschte, ging vorüber. An der Gelehrtenkonferenz in Uscha, da das Patriarchat und das Synhedrion wiederentstehen, nahm Rabbi Meir hervorragenden Anteil und wirkte dann als Chacham an der Seite des Patriarchen Rabbi Schimon ben Gamliel II.

Zwischen Rabbi Meir, dem hervorragendsten Gelehrten des Zeitalters, und dem ihm im Amte vorgesetzten Patriarchen kam es jedoch zu einem Konflikt. Rabbi Schimon, der die Autorität seines Amtes festigen wollte, hatte beschlossen, die Gleichheit, die bisher zwischen dem Patriarchen und den anderen Würdenträgern bestand, durch Einführung unterschiedlicher Formen der Ehrenbezeigung aufzuheben. In Abwesenheit des Chachams Rabbi Meir und des Gerichtspräsidenten Rabbi Natan führte der Patriarch die neue Rangordnung ein, die ihn als Fürsten öffentlich auszeichnen sollte. Als die zurückgesetzten Würdenträger, der an Gelehrsamkeit den Patriarchen übertrafen, von der hervorstechenden Rangordnung des politischen Amtsträgers über die Gelehrten erfuhren, sprach Rabbi Meir zu Rabbi Natan: „Ich bin Chacham und du bist Gerichtspräsident, wollen wir etwas gegen ihn unternehmen, wie es gegen uns getan hat. Ich will mich gegen ihn unternehmen? Wir wollen ihn aufforden, den Traktat Ukzin vorzutragen, dessen er nicht kundig ist, und da es auch nicht können wird ... seine Leistung mit ihm absetzen. Ich hörte Rabbi Jakob ben Kodschi, und er sagte: Rabbi helfe und bewahre, in Beschämung geraten. Da ging er und setzte sich hinter die Söller des Rabbi Schimon ben Gamliel, und lernte und wiederholte. Den Traktat Ukzin — lernte und wiederholte. Da sprach Rabbi Schimon: Was soll dies bedeuten, vielleicht hat sich, hebüte und bewahre, etwas im Lehrhause ereignet? Da richtete er seine Aufmerksamkeit darauf und lernte nun. Am folgenden Tage sprachen Rabbi Natan und Rabbi Meir zu ihm: Möge doch der Meister kommen und uns aus dem Traktat Ukzin vortragen. Da begann er und trug vor. Nachdem er geendigt hatte, sprach er zu ihnen: Hätte ich ihn nicht gelernt, so würdet ihr mich der Beschämung ausgesetzt haben. Da befahl er, und man wies sie aus dem Lehrhause. Hierauf schrieben sie ihre (wissenschaftlichen) Fragen auf und warfen sie ins Lehrhaus; würden sie beantwortet, so waren sie erledigt, und wurden sie nicht beantwortet, so schrieben sie auch die Antworten auf und warfen sie hinein. Da sprach Rabbi Jose: Die Tora ist draußen und wir drinnen! Da ordnete Rabbi Schimon ben Gamliel an, daß man sie wieder einlasse, jedoch bestrafe, daß man keine Lehre in ihrem Namen vortrage. Alsdann wurde Rabbi Meir mit der Bezeichnung „Andere sagen" und Rabbi Natan mit der Bezeichnung

„Manche sagen" belegt. Hierauf sagte man ihnen im Traume, daß sie hingehen und Abbitte leisten sollen. Rabbi Natan ging hin, Rabbi Meir aber ging nicht hin, denn er sagte, Träume nützen nicht und schaden nicht.

Das Zerwürfnis mit dem Patriarchen, das in dieser Episode zum Ausbruch kam, ging offenbar auf einen Streit der Methoden zurück. Im Gegensatz zu den Patriarchen, der sich dem Spiele des Theoretisierens und der dialektischen Forschungsart widersetzte, führte Rabbi Meir Phantasie und Scharfsinn in den Lehrbetrieb ein, was das in einem solchen Maße nie zuvor der Fall gewesen war. Die Kasuistik, deren Anfänge älter waren, entwickelte bei ihm bis zur Virtuosität, als ob ein Selbstzweck der Bildung wäre. „Wer Rabbi Meir im Lehrhaus sah, dem schien es, als ob Berge entwurzelt und aneinandergerieben würden." Diese methodische Eigenart trug auch nicht nur segensvolle Früchte; sie artete bei seinen Schülern in eine Leidenschaft zur Sophistik aus. Die Jünger galten als streitsüchtig und wirkten so, als ob nicht das Studium der Tora, sondern das Niederkämpfung der Gegner im Ziel wäre.

Dieser Tatbestand hatte einen tragischen Einfluß auf das Schicksal Rabbi Meirs. „Offenbar und bekannt ist es dem, durch dessen Wort die Welt erschaffen wurde, daß im Zeitalter Rabbi Meirs niemand gewesen ist, der ihm gleichgekommen wäre; nur deshalb setzten die Weisen die Entscheidungen nicht nach seiner Lehre fest, weil sie nicht in die Tiefe seiner Gedanken zu dringen vermochten. Er erklärte nämlich das Unreine für rein und begründete es, und ebenso das Reine für unrein und begründete es."

Rabbi Meir wollte sich vor dem Patriarchen nicht beugen und verhärtte in seinem Widerstande. Nunmehr enwog der Patriarch, den Bann über Rabbi Meir zu verhängen. Rabbi Meir verließ das Heilige Land, der es liebte, und begab sich nach Asia, wo er die Lehren Rabbi Meirs von Lehem zubrachte. Der Patriarch hat seinen Groll gegen den Mann, der „die Würde des Patriarchenhauses untergraben wollte", nicht überwunden. Man trug die Lehren Rabbi Meirs vor, jedoch nicht in seinem Namen. Selbst der Sohn Rabbi Schimons, Rabbi Jehuda Hanasi, „der sehr sanftmütig war", erinnerte an den Ausdruck „Rabbi Meir sagte".

„Als Rabbi Meir das Buch Hiob beendet hatte, sagte er folgendes: Das Ende des Menschen ist das Sterben, das Ende des Viehes das Schlachten, und alles ist für den Tod bestimmt. Heil dem, der in der Tora groß wird, sich mit der Tora abmüht, seinem Schöpfer Annehmlichkeiten bereitet, mit gutem Namen aufgewachsen und mit gutem Namen aus der Welt geschieden ist."

Im Schöpfungsbericht heißt es: Und siehe, es war sehr gut, das ist der Tod, erläutert Rabbi Meir.

Aus Legende und Gleichnis
Die Honigwabe

Nach dem wunderbaren Durchzug durch das Schilfmeer führte der Weg die Kinder Israel einige Tage am Ufer entlang; linker Hand lag die Wasserwüste, rechter Hand die Sandwüste, und sie verschmachteten vor Hunger und Durst. Da fand ein Mann im Sande eine Honigwabe und brachte sie dem Mose. Allein Mose nahm die Wabe und warf sie ins Wasser. Es gab ihm Zorn von mir, daß ich nur mein Leben zu erhalten suchte und die Leute um mich herum sterben sähe." Da stürzten sich einige von den Mannen ins Meer, um die Honigwabe zu erhaschen; jedoch erschöpft vor Schwäche. Die Tür sich allein sich hatten setzen wollen, mußten eines angstvollen Todes sterben. Die aber brachen frei, hatten Israels verblichen, zogen weiter, hin ins Gelobte Land. Gott sandte ihnen Wachteln und Manna, sie stillten Hunger und Durst, und ein Geist hebte wieder auf.

Fig. 3. The essay on Rabbi Meir in the *Gemeindeblatt*, May 17, 1936.

humility and reverence for God and enables him to be just, pious, upright, and loyal. . . . Further, it grants him kingship, authority, and investigative power in law. The secrets of Torah are revealed to him. He becomes like a spring that never dries up and a stream that grows unceasingly. He is called modest, patient, and forbearing."[119]

These words, which flow from the depths of consciousness, are an expression of spiritual power. Coming from Rabbi Meir, "the Illuminator," "who illuminated the eyes of the wise in *halachah*," they seem like propositions stemming from his own experience, rather than principles of unqualified factuality.[120] He taught, "The sages have given the same power to their words as to the Torah." Even more strongly than claims for the majesty of the scholar and of the catharsis, yes, holiness effected by Torah, what touches us here is the awareness of the magic of the spirit, the fullness of grace accorded by the study of the Law.

Rabbi Meir was one of the most influential men to further the shaping of the Teaching, and through the power of his methodology and imagination he triggered a productive continuation of talmudic study. Thanks to his systemization of traditional material, he made possible the subsequent compilation of the Mishnah.[121]

In his youth he was admitted to Rabbi Akiba's House of Learning. Since he did not yet know enough to be able to follow Rabbi Akiba's keen-minded lectures, he switched to Rabbi Ishmael, where he deepened his store of learning, after which he returned to Rabbi Akiba, whose commentary he now understood and by whom he was then ordained. He went from teacher to teacher and learned the different schools and ways of teaching.[122]

On the side he worked as a scribe. He wrote "beautifully and splendidly." The ink he used, derived from a chemical mixture that he introduced to the Jews, was especially long lasting and glossy.[123] The Torah scrolls from his pen were particularly sought after, and he was lauded as "a sage and a scribe."[124] Of the three shekels that his work brought in every week, he spent one-third on food and one-third on clothing, and one-third he gave to impoverished scholars. "Rabbi, how will your children manage if you spend the earnings from your writing on the poor?" his students asked. "If they are virtuous," he replied, "they will fulfill the words of the psalm: 'I have never seen a righteous man abandoned' (Psalm 37:25). And if they are not virtuous, why should I bequeath my property to God's enemies?"[125]

His renowned wife, Beruria, the daughter of the martyr Rabbi Haninah ben Teradion, was also learned and pious. Once when Rabbi Meir was in the House of Learning, both his sons died. Their mother carried them into the adjacent room and covered them with a blanket. After sunset Rabbi Meir returned home and asked about his sons. "They went to the House of Learning," Beruria replied. "I looked for them, but in vain," said Rabbi Meir. Beruria handed him the wine cup and he gave the blessing for the end of the Sabbath. Again he asked about his sons. Beruria tried to calm him, saying "they went out and will be back home soon," and she placed food and drink before him. After the meal she began, "Rabbi, one question: A long time ago someone entrusted me with a valuable possession, and today he demanded it back. Should I give it to him?" Outraged, Rabbi Meir answered,

"What?! You would refuse to return an entrusted security to its owner?" "Only with your permission," answered Beruria, taking him by the hand into the adjacent room and pulling the blanket away. Horrified, Rabbi Meir saw the bodies of his two sons and called out, weeping, "My sons, my teachers, you have enlightened me with your wisdom." He wailed and lamented. "What's this?" said Beruria to him. "Didn't you say that it was one's duty to return an entrusted security to its owner without complaint? God has given this to us, God has taken it from us, and we shall praise His Name."[126]

As a young man Rabbi Meir had earned much respect, but also much opposition. He was popular as a lecturer and famous as a writer of fables. Not only was his playfulness expressed in his three hundred fox fables,[127] but the dialectical imagination he brought to the study of the law also had the impact of a spiritual suggestion. When it was necessary he could appear in the guise of a Roman knight.[128] Self-confident, excitable, and perhaps willful, he sometimes enjoyed provoking his sober and cautious contemporaries. He learned "Torah from the mouth of Aher"[129]—the universally damned apostate. When flames erupted from Aher's grave, he extinguished them with his coat. His friends asked him, "If you were in the Beyond, whom would you rather visit—your father or your teacher?" He answered, "First my father, and then my teacher."[130]

The Hadrianic persecutions also had an impact on Rabbi Meir's personal life. But, as he told it, the time came when listening spies no longer forced him to go to the roof to softly recite the *Shema*, or read the Megillah at night or the Torah on the Sabbath. At the meeting of scholars in Usha that constituted the patriarchate and the Sanhedrin, Rabbi Meir played a significant role, acting as *hacham* [chief sage] at the side of the patriarch, Rabbi Shimon ben Gamliel II.[131]

But a conflict arose between Rabbi Meir, the outstanding scholar of the time, and the patriarch, who was his superior in office. Rabbi Shimon, who wanted to reinforce the authority of his office, had decided to introduce different forms of honorifics in order to eliminate the equality that had existed until then between the patriarch and other officials. In the absence of Rabbi Meir, the *hacham*, and Rabbi Natan, the court president, the patriarch introduced the new hierarchy with which he gave himself the rank of Prince. When the now lower-ranking officials— whose learning exceeded that of the patriarch—heard of the elevation in rank of the political official over the scholars, Rabbi Meir said to Rabbi Natan: "I am *hacham* and you are court president. Shall we undertake something against him, as he has done to us? What action shall we undertake? Let's demand that he discuss the tractate Uktzin,[132] which he doesn't know, and since he won't be able to do it, we can dismiss him. I will then be court president, and you will be prince." When Rabbi Jacob ben Korshai heard this, he said, "He will, God forbid, be shamed." Then he left and sat behind Rabbi Shimon ben Gamliel's balcony, studied the tractate Uktzin and studied it again, studied and studied again. Then Rabbi Shimon said: What can this mean? Maybe, God forbid, something happened in the House of Learning. Then he grew attentive and began to study along with him.

The next day Rabbi Natan and Rabbi Meir said to him: The Master should come and discuss the tractate Uktzin with us. So he began to discuss it. When he had finished, he said to them: If I hadn't studied it, you would have exposed me to shame. And so he ordered them expelled from the House of Learning.

Hereupon they wrote down their (scholarly) questions and tossed them into the House of Learning. If they were answered, that took care of it; if they were not answered, they would write down the answers and throw them in. Then Rabbi Jose said: The Torah is outside and we are inside! So Rabbi Shimon ben Gamliel ordered that they be let in, but that they be punished by allowing no teaching to be presented in their name. After this Rabbi Meir was given the designation "Others say" and Rabbi Natan the designation "Some say." Thereupon they were told in a dream that they should go and apologize. Rabbi Natan went, but Rabbi Meir did not, because he said that dreams neither helped nor harmed.[133]

The enmity between Rabbi Meir and the patriarch during this episode apparently grew out of a methodological disagreement. In contrast to the patriarch, who opposed the play of theorizing and dialectical querying, Rabbi Meir introduced into teaching an unprecedented degree of *imagination* and *acuity of intelligence*. He developed casuistry—in itself nothing new—into an art of such virtuosity that it seemed the goal of learning, an end unto itself. "Anyone who saw Rabbi Meir in the House of Learning felt as if he were seeing mountains uprooted and rubbed against one another."[134] This methodological characteristic did not yield only positive results; among his students it developed into a passion for sophistry. His disciples earned a reputation for picking fights and behaving as if their goal were not the study of Torah but the crushing of their opponents.[135]

This state of affairs had tragic consequences for Rabbi Meir's fate. "It was obvious and well known to Him whose word created the world that in Rabbi Meir's time no one was his equal. The wise decided against his decisions only because they were unable to penetrate into the depths of his thinking, for he would declare the impure as pure, and substantiate it, and similarly the pure as impure, and substantiate that."[136]

Rabbi Meir did not want to yield to the patriarch and remained obdurate in his resistance. Finally, the patriarch considered whether to excommunicate Rabbi Meir. Rabbi Meir left the Holy Land, which he loved, and went to Asia,[137] where he spent the rest of his life. The patriarch never got over his anger against the man who "wanted to undermine the dignity of the House of the Patriarch." Rabbi Meir's teachings were passed along without naming him.[138] Even Rabbi Shimon's son, Rabbi Judah Hanasi, "who was very humble," avoided the expression, "Rabbi Meir said."[139]

"When Rabbi Meir had finished the book of Job, he said the following: The end of a person is death, the end of an animal is slaughter, and everything is destined for death. Honor to him who struggles with the Torah, who strives to please God, who grows up with a good name and departs from the world with a good name."[140]

In the story of Creation we read: And see, it was very good. "That is death," adds Rabbi Meir.[141]

Rabbi Judah Hanasi

Rabbi Judah Hanasi was the son of Rabbi Shimon ben Gamliel II, so he, too, traced his ancestry back to Hillel, and from there, back to King David. He succeeded his father in the year 165 CE. Although he came from a long line of Rabbis who held the office of *nasi*, he is the only one to be called "Hanasi" (the *nasi*), and the only one to be referred to simply as "Rabbi."

The great accomplishment of Rabbi Judah Hanasi's career was his codification of the Mishnah. Heschel mentioned contributions to this project in three earlier essays: Rabbi Akiba "created the first outlines of a system," Rabbi Shimon ben Gamliel II "prepared the way" by "giving priority to knowledge over intellectual brilliance," and Rabbi Meir's "systemization of traditional material . . . made possible the subsequent compilation of the Mishnah." But it was Rabbi Judah Hanasi who unified the various strands into a lasting product.

Heschel compares the reception of the Mishnah with that of Maimonides's *Mishneh Torah*, the code of Jewish law published in 1180. Unlike the Mishnah of Judah Hanasi, the *Mishneh Torah* met with fierce opposition. Many of its critics objected to the ways it differed from the Mishnah: Maimonides did not include minority decisions, nor did he cite the names of the sages whose opinions he recorded. Maimonides had hoped that because his work provided answers instead of complex discussions, it would make the study of Talmud unnecessary for most Jews. Though the *Mishneh Torah* is an undisputed classic, it did not succeed in that goal. The Mishnah of Rabbi Judah Hanasi succeeded not by overcoming but by preserving the dialogic character of the Oral Law, albeit now in written form.

This essay was first published in the *Gemeindeblatt der jüdischen Gemeinde zu Berlin* on May 31, 1936.

The emergence of Rabbi Judah Hanasi was a golden moment in the history of the Jewish person. His contemporaries, who called him simply "Rabbi," sensed in him perfection and grace. They said, "If the hoped-for Messiah should turn up among the living, it will surely be Rabbi."[142] He knew how to administer with piety the authority that is inherent in life itself. The respect he was accorded benefited both the nation and history and made it possible for him to realize the outcome that was consistent with spiritual development. His character and way of life, which were the basis of his authority, were, at their core, a much more significant achievement than whatever deeds he accomplished.

He emanated an aura of a unique sacral-aristocratic solemnity. He lived his life in a completely Jewish manner, in the style of a Jewish prince, characterized by outer splendor and inner asceticism. As he was dying he was supposed to have pointed his ten fingers upward and said, "Lord of the world, it is clear and obvious to you that with my ten fingers I have worn myself out in the Torah and that not even with my little finger did I enjoy any earthly pleasure."[143] And yet he, who had been on friendly terms with a Roman emperor,[144] headed a princely court. People entertained the orientally exaggerated fantasy that "the Rabbi's stable master was wealthier than the Persian King Shabor."[145]

Deep ambivalence and duality characterize his essence. He was, at heart, gentle, but his manner could be strict to the point of hardness. Required by his position to be rigorous, he tried to use the law to soften burdensome regulations and to suspend outdated customs. He had the dignity of a prince and the freshness of a sensitive heart. He was often moved to tears, and then he cried like a child.[146] His strength lay not in emotion or imagination but in intellect and will, in political insight and drive.

He descended from Davidic nobility,[147] and after the death of his father, Rabbi Shimon ben Gamliel II, he was next in line for the patriarchy and thus for the directorship of the central House of Learning and the High Court.

"Conduct the office of prince with dignity and cast bile among the disciples."[148] Based on these principles, which he had formulated, his princely office attained a previously unknown authority under his administration. He tolerated no inappropriate aspersions against himself and was not afraid of resorting to severe measures when it came to defending the dignity of his office.

He decreed that no one could make legal decisions without express permission.[149] During Rabbi's period in office, the consecration of a teacher of the law or judge, which until then could be performed by any teacher of the law, became the exclusive prerogative of the patriarch, and it could be exercised even without consulting the Collegial Court. A nomination by the Collegial Court without the patriarch's confirmation was invalid.[150] Official appointments, both secular and religious, were thus dependent on Rabbi, who, indeed, exercised utmost restraint in granting ordination.

A benefactor on a grand scale, he supported numerous disciples from home and abroad who were studying at the academies of the Holy Land. He was a generous patron and teacher, but he was also free of all smugness. "I have learned much from my teachers, still more from my colleagues, but most of all from my students," he is supposed to have sometimes said.[151]

The psychological underside of his respect for scholars was apparent in his disrespect for the so-called *am ha'aretz*—the ordinary people. He thought that all the world's misfortune was caused by the *am ha'aretz*.[152] When, during the years of famine, he opened his abundantly stocked granaries, in his arrogance he made it expressly known that only those who studied the Bible, the Mishnah, the Talmud,[153] *halachah* or *aggadah* would be allowed to enter. Ordinary people, however, would not be admitted. A contemporary scholar tried very discretely to remedy this hubris. Rabbi Jonatan ben Amram appeared before the patriarch and said, "Rabbi, feed me." Rabbi asked him, "Have you read the Bible?" "No," Rabbi Jonatan answered. "If that's the case, how can I feed you?" "Feed me like a dog or a raven." After Rabbi Jonatan had left, Rabbi was very angry. "Oh, how I regret giving bread to someone from *am ha'aretz*." Then his son said, "Might it have been your student Jonatan ben Amran, who does not want to profit from the honor paid to the Torah?" Later inquiries confirmed this suggestion. Then Rabbi said, "Everyone may enter!"[154]

He was very self-confident and intent on maintaining his princely dignity. Nonetheless, it was precisely his modesty for which he was admired. "With the death of the Rabbi humility and aversion to sin ceased to exist."[155] This entered the collective memory of the people.

Even as a young man, he gained respect as a scholar. "We drink his water," even his teachers confessed, and his father said to him, "You are a lion, the son of a fox."[156] His influence also extended over the lands of the diaspora. Even in distant Babylonia no one could perform an official duty without Rabbi's authorization.[157] In spite of his position as sole ruler and a severity that could sometimes be very hard indeed, unlike his father and grandfather he had no rivals. "Never since Moses have scholarliness and authority come together as they have with Rabbi."[158] His "handsomeness, strength, wealth, honor, and wisdom" were admired.[159] "He who sees Rabbi—or King Solomon—in a dream, may hope for wisdom," was the teaching of talmudic dream interpretation.[160]

An unyielding seriousness formed his life. Supposedly he slept for no longer than sixty breaths.[161] From him there arose a metaphysical idea of the individual that became highly significant for Jewish life and thought. "On a day on which Rabbi laughed the world was doomed."[162]

"Once a calf was led to the slaughter. It hid its head in the corner of the Rabbi's coat and cried. And Rabbi said to it: Go on, you were created for this purpose. Thereupon it was decided in heaven that, because he had shown no mercy, he should suffer. His suffering lasted for thirteen years. For six years he suffered from bladder stones and for seven years from scurvy. One day the Rabbi's maid was cleaning his room. A weasel's young were lying there, and she swept them out, too. Then Rabbi said to her, 'Spare them, for it is written: His mercy is upon all His works' (Psalm 145:9). Thereupon it was decided in heaven, 'Because he was merciful, we shall show mercy to him.'"[163]

The position of power he attained made it possible for him to work the soil of Jewish life as with a harrow, breaking the clumps and removing the weeds. He eliminated major customs governing the dating and proclaiming of the calendar;[164] he eased the laws of the jubilee year[165] and tithes and determined that it was not necessary to tithe the fruits of certain Palestinian border areas.[166]

His plans for far-reaching reform roused the representatives of rigid conservatism into action. "His brothers and his father's entire family joined forces and said to him, 'You decree that entering a place that your forefathers held to be forbidden is now permitted?!' Thereupon Rabbi answered decisively: 'My forefathers left me an opportunity to earn distinction.'"[167] He was even about to eliminate the laws of the sabbatical year entirely. But Rabbi Pinchas ben Yair, who was esteemed as a saint, prevented it.[168]

The structure of the Oral Teaching was badly damaged by the storms of history. The austere, moldy traditions, which had been transmitted in every generation, were rent asunder and splintered as a result of wars, persecutions, banishments, and "diminishing spiritual strength." Piece by piece the Oral Teaching had to be rebuilt through assiduous study of the Torah, in whose words the traditions were indicated. For this reason, the restored teachings usually had the form of *midrash*, the explanation and the discussion of biblical verses. Efforts had long been undertaken to free them from their dependence on the biblical text and to crystallize them as decisions and norms—as *Mishnah*. Since the founding of the Academy in Yavne, scholars had been collecting the principles and organizing them into various tractates, in which legal issues were presented. These collections were not made public but rather were intended only for the private use of teachers and lecturers.

The hindrances and impediments in oral transmission

were significantly exacerbated by a powerful surge in the study of the law. The abundance of laws that, since Hillel's time, had blossomed out of the ground of tradition exceeded the memory's ability to absorb it. The canonization of traditional material had become a question of survival. But the written form contradicted the very essence of the Oral Teaching, which had found conscious and religiously sanctioned expression in the prohibition from being put in writing.[169]

Rabbi's decision to redact, write down and publish the entire Oral Teaching as a canonical work of Judaism was both bold and wonderful. It was said in a later era, "Where it was important to act for the Lord, they broke your law."[170] The carrying out of this intention did indeed signify a spiritual revolution.

The old dispute over methods now announced itself as a dispute over form—the balanced form of the rule, of the Mishnah, or the fluid form of discussion, of midrash. For generations midrash had been preferred to Mishnah. Rabbi himself initially preferred midrash. But then he decided once and for all on *synthesis*, on Mishnah, and undertook a systematizing of the entire body of teaching that had been transmitted to him (excepting a few attempts) piecemeal and scattered, and brought everything together into a finely conceptualized coherent form, into one unified whole.

The ripe crop of the centuries stood high, and all were reluctant to tear the fruit from its natural soil. Rabbi Judah Hanasi, who had the most productive mind and the bravest heart of the talmudic age, summoned the courage to harvest it, and to build the silo that became the Mishnah, in which he gathered the yield of many generations. This container held rich provisions for the millennia, and they are preserved there to this day.

The exertions of the patriarchal dynasty (from which Rabbi descended) to oppose the vigorous efforts of particularism[171] using the patriarch's and the Sanhedrin's positions of power found their conclusion in Rabbi's activity. The Mishnah became the bearer of *spiritual unity*, and ultimately it rendered the office of the patriarchate, to which it owed its existence, superfluous.

For Rabbi stepped back from his work. The self-imposed limitations to his role as author that he exercised in every regard, the distance he kept from traditions that he rendered whenever possible in their received wording, style of disputation, existing arrangement, and with the precise naming of their source, his forgoing of stylization, despite his puritanical and masterful feel for language, his renunciation of an absolute systematizing despite his fine sense for composition—all this showed the nobility of his being.

Even more than his creative inspiration and his scholarly activity, it is the success of the Mishnah, its quickly won acceptance by people throughout the diaspora, that marks the significance of his achievement. Maimonides's project—much less bold and a thousand years later—was not able to prevail. The Mishnah attained a respect that far exceeded Rabbi's goal. It pushed all other collections aside and became a code of law and almost the sole source for study.

The personal condition that made this possible was the holy authority of the patriarch. To have attained this authority is the glory of his life.

Rabbi Hiyya

The first seven "Personalities" essays followed a steady pattern of publication in the *Gemeindeblatt der jüdischen Gemeinde zu Berlin*: one article every two or three weeks, from Rabbi Johanan ben Zakkai on February 23 to Rabbi Judah Hanasi on May 31, 1936. Then eleven weeks went by before the final installment appeared in the August 16 edition.

The subject of this eighth and final essay, Rabbi Hiyya, is an outlier as well. He is less well known than the others. And while the first seven essays form a neat set, beginning and ending with the events that define the mishnaic period—the destruction of the Second Temple in 70 CE and the codification of the Mishnah in around 200 CE—Rabbi Hiyya's career followed the close of the Mishnah. He died around 230 CE.[172]

In his later years, Rabbi Hiyya returned with his sons from the exhilic community in Babylonia to teach Torah in Palestine. Heschel notices a repeating trope in the Jewish narrative, appearing also in the stories of Ezra in the fifth century BCE and of Hillel in the first century BCE, both of whom move from an intellectually rich life in Babylonia to a Palestine in need of learning. The same push and pull between diaspora and home plays an important role in the intellectual and spiritual life of the Jews, stretching as far back as the story of Abraham, who also leaves Babylonia for the land of Canaan.

Rabbi Hiyya's significant contribution to the development of the Oral Law was collecting and recording Rabbinic dicta that were not included in the Mishnah. For generations to come, the work of reconciling his *baraitot* (outside things) with the sayings collected by Rabbi Judah Hanasi would help to fuel the engine of talmudic discourse. By ending his series with Rabbi Hiyya, Heschel leaves his readers with the understanding that the new post-temple Judaism invented by the Rabbis will continue to grow and change.

The Jews in Palestine—ordinary people as well as scholars—lived in fear that the Torah could be lost to them. They lost their land, their leaders had been killed and all security had been taken from them. Most of them were refugees, emigrants, and martyrs. Their children could not be schooled, and it was almost impossible to maintain the colleges for judges and teachers. Misery hung over them. . . . "The Torah would almost have been forgotten—had Rabbi Hiyya not appeared!"[173]

The circumstances in Palestine had changed. Gradually the country recovered from the rebellions and wars. An intellectual life began to stir. From Babylonia—which until recently had been home to a massive emigration from Palestine—many Jews now came to participate in the rebuilding of the Holy Land. It was at this time that the well-respected Rabbi Hiyya—sometimes known as Rabbi Hiyya the Great—came to Palestine with his sons.

His arrival was an epochal event and was regarded as providential. He was compared with the great historic figures, with Ezra and Hillel, who, like him, had come from Babylonia to "renew the Torah."[174] His particular humanity determined the uniqueness of his achievements, which in turn formed the basis of his historic significance.

Rabbi Hiyya loved the small things. For him minor duties were significant. He concerned himself with the activities that were most disregarded by others. What mattered to him were mundane matters in the here and now. He had no need to spin out theories to learned students. He did not use the large fortune he had brought from Babylonia to found an academy and host disciples from many countries, nor was he a patron of legal scholars. Rather, he was a supporter of sages and beginners.

He went to the provinces, moving from city to city to teach small children the alphabet. "I grow flax and weave nets, then I catch deer and give their meat to the hungry to eat, and prepare parchment scrolls from their skins. Then I go to the east, where there are no teachers for the children, and I copy out the five books of the Torah for five children and teach six children the six orders of the Mishnah. Then I instruct each of them to teach his order to his friends."[175]

This simple, very unceremonious manner and the calm of his kindness were characteristic of him. He had the stature of a master, but he subordinated himself to his contemporary, the prince, Rabbi Judah Hanasi.

Living at the same time as Rabbi Judah Hanasi, Rabbi Hiyya found his effectiveness and influence limited. Rabbi Hiyya's achievements and the national and intellectual milieu in which he lived were perhaps really similar to Ezra's and Hillel's. But while they could meet the challenges of their time independently, the prince, Rabbi Judah, was working in the Holy Land as Rabbi Hiyya's contemporary.

He refrained, it seems, from engaging in any position of leadership. He held no office and assumed no public honors. His relationship to Rabbi Judah Hanasi was very problematic. Since Rabbi Hiyya was famous, and in no way inferior in learning, Rabbi Judah Hanasi had to regard him not as a student but as an equal. But apparently collegiality was not the prince's style.

Humility was not merely a feature of Rabbi Hiyya's

personality, but rather his essence. Not only his manner and his attitudes but his life's very structure derived from his modesty. A contemporary once articulated his sense of superiority to Rabbi Hiyya by saying that if the Torah were ever to be forgotten in Israel, he would restore it himself with his keen intellect. "And I," responded Rabbi Hiyya, "am seeing to it that the Torah will *not* be forgotten in Israel."[176]

The scholars were scornful of the *am ha'aretz*, while Rabbi Hiyya loved them and dedicated his teachings to them. The aristocrat Rabbi Hanasi insisted on exclusivity when teaching Torah. Rabbi Hiyya taught publicly in the open. This earned him the anger of the patriarch, who had given the order not to teach in the streets: "As the hips are hidden, so are the words of the Torah." When the patriarch learned that Rabbi Hiyya was nevertheless teaching in the streets, he became very annoyed and punished him: for thirty days Rabbi Hiyya was not allowed to visit the patriarch.[177]

Rabbi Judah Hanasi had collected the most important teachings and brought them together into a legal compilation, the *Mishnah*. Rabbi Hiyya focused on the mass of teachings that had not gotten official recognition and had not been taken up into the tractates of the Mishnah. He gleaned laboriously and collected neglected material, but he did not construct a new system. Instead he organized the "left out tenets" into a supplemental work, the *Tosefta*, maintaining the structure of the Mishnah, though the Tosefta was larger.

He did not strive for authority. He had no interest in achievement as a personal accomplishment, but only as it concerned the matter itself. His life was poor in external luster—both at home and in public. "His wife tormented Rabbi Hiyya. Nevertheless, when he found something for her, it was his habit to wrap it in his handkerchief and to bring it to her. When his nephew said to him, 'But she is tormenting the Master,' he replied, 'It is enough that she raises our children and protects us from sin.'"[178] But another time he said to his nephew, "May the All-Merciful One protect you from that which is worse than death," by which he was alluding to this verse: "I find woman more bitter than death" (Ecclesiastes 7:26).[179]

Rabbi Hiyya's actions were the fulfillment of goodness: they earned him no reward—no power, no honors. "His achievements were useful to the whole world, but not to himself."[180] Rabbi Judah Hanasi—who applied the verse to him, "From a distant land the Lord summoned the man to advise me,"[181] by which he meant, "How significant is Hiyya's work!"[182]—nonetheless demanded of him complete subordination. Even the patriarch's son expected deference from Rabbi Hiyya. He complained to his father when Rabbi Hiyya did not stand up before him in the bathhouse.[183]

The following anecdote is characteristic of his relationship to possessions in life. He said to his wife, "If a poor man comes to you, bring him bread so that bread will also be brought to your children." And she said to him, "You are cursing them." He responded, "A wheel turns around in the world."[184]

In contrast to Rabbi Judah Hanasi, Rabbi Hiyya was not accorded a holy title, but his power in prayer was said to surpass that of the Prince. It is told that the angel

Elijah used to spend time in Rabbi's House of Learning. Once, on the day of the new moon, Elijah was delayed and didn't arrive at the usual time. When he finally appeared, Rabbi asked him: Why is the Master late? He answered: It took a while until I had gotten Abraham up, washed his hands and then, after he prayed, laid him down again, and then the same with Isaac and the same with Jacob. I thought they might pray too fervently for mercy and make the Messiah arrive before his time. Then Rabbi asked him: Is there anyone like them in this world? Elijah answered: There are Rabbi Hiyya and his sons. Thereupon Rabbi decreed a day of fasting[185] and summoned Rabbi Hiyya and his sons to the prayer leader's podium. When Rabbi Hiyya said the second blessing of the *Amidah*—"Who causes the wind to blow"—a wind began to blow, and when he said "and the rain to fall," rain fell, and when he then continued, "who calls the dead to immortal life," the universe moved. And in heaven they said: Who has revealed the secret to the world? Then Rabbi Hiyya was punished and his prayer remained unfinished.[186]

"Ever since Rabbi Hiyya and his sons have come from exile to Palestine, lightning bolts, earthquakes, hurricanes, and thunder have ceased, wine no longer turns sour, and [pests] no longer destroy the flax."[187]

PART 3

Don Yitzhak Abravanel

Context

Don Yitzhak Abravanel (1437–1509) was a respected statesman and scholar, a man of wealth and influence at the highest levels of medieval European society—both Jewish and non-Jewish. Over the course of his career he served six kings in four kingdoms. But while his skills in finance and politics were greatly valued by the royalty and nobility of Portugal, Spain, and Italy, he served at their whim. The favor he found in their courts was fragile, dependent on the results of power struggles beyond his control. During his lifetime the Jews of the Iberian Peninsula were to undergo some of the most terrible persecutions in history, and the limited protection that his special relationships would afford him could not even begin to save them.

Heschel's biography of Abravanel was commissioned on the heels of his well-received book on Maimonides. He used the opportunity to delve further into his interest in medieval Jewish thought, while at the same time producing a powerful educational offering for German Jews. Like his *Gemeindeblatt* essays on the Rabbis, this work teaches history as though it were as timely as the latest news.

After the brief preface, the first section presents a sketch of Abravanel's life. Heschel follows Don Yitzhak's travels from Portugal to Spain and then to Italy at the end of the fifteenth century and the beginning of the sixteenth century, as the Renaissance was transforming medieval Europe. The distributed power hierarchy of the feudal system was yielding to the consolidated rule of monarchs, while smaller kingdoms became prey to the larger powers, France and Spain. In the cultural realm, the scholasticism of medieval intellectual life was giving way to humanism. Heschel shows Abravanel in the roles of both player and pawn as these changes unfold.

The second, third, and fourth sections examine Abravanel's responses to the major philosophical issues that were salient at the juncture of medieval and Renaissance culture: Is the world eternal, or did it come into being at a particular moment, through an act of God's will? Does existence have a purpose, a fulfillment toward which everything aims? Will there be a Messianic Age, when time as we know it ceases to be?

Many of the issues engaging Abravanel had been made central to the Jewish conversation three hundred years earlier by the great Jewish philosopher and physician Moses Maimonides (1138–1204), also known as "the Ramban." Maimonides lived in Spain under Muslim rule and was immersed in the scientific scholarship of his time, namely the study of Aristotle and other Greek thinkers whose works had been brought to Europe by Islamic scholars. Through the intellectually compelling Aristotelian images of a rational universe completely understandable by the human mind, Maimonides discovered a new way to think about the God of the Jewish tradition.

The focus of Jewish philosophy in the medieval era was the attempt to reconcile Jewish tradition and the rational science of the time. In the centuries following the publication of Maimonides's *Mishneh Torah* (1180) and *Guide of the Perplexed* (1190), the so-called "Maimonidean Controversies" raged. In his *Mishneh Torah*, Maimonides provided a straightforward summary of Jewish law that some saw as an arrogant attempt to supersede the Talmud, obviating the need for its intricate arguments and replacing them with clear and distinct summaries. In *Guide of the Perplexed*, he laid out philosophical positions with roots in Greek thought that some saw as deep challenges to traditional Jewish beliefs. Supporters of Maimonides welcomed the rationalist turn in Jewish thought, while his critics disparaged his ideas as heretical. The debate was not civil—there were mutual excommunications; books were banned and even burned.

Heschel presents a complex picture of the relationship between Abravanel's thought and Maimonides's legacy. Despite reservations, Abravanel studied Maimonides carefully and wrote a commentary on his most philosophically complex work, the *Guide of the Perplexed*. He defended Maimonides against his critics, believing they had misunderstood the depth of Maimonides's discussions and had therefore advocated what might be called thin compromise positions.

As an example of an area in which Maimonides held a principled position that was watered down by later thinkers, Heschel brings the question of the role of dogmatic belief in Judaism. Maimonides lays out thirteen principles about which a Jew must achieve philosophical understanding and true belief in order to attain life in the world to come. These include the existence, unity, incorporeality, and eternity of God; the truth of prophecy; the eventual coming of the Messiah; and the resurrection of the dead. Abravanel defended this position against the attacks of two later thinkers: Hasdai Crescas (ca. 1340–1410), the chief rabbi of the Jewish community of Aragon and a critic of the application of Aristotelian rationalism to Jewish theology; and Joseph Albo (died 1444), a student of Crescas. For Crescas and Albo, the need to believe certain dogmas placed a limit on the extent to which the Jew was permitted to engage in philosophical speculation. The Jewish philosopher was free to enjoy research up to a point, but if that research threatened to undermine belief in any of three primary tenets, one must desist rather than risk conflict with religious doctrine. For Maimonides, on the other hand, the thirteen principles played a completely different role. They were not commanded stopping points past which one was not permitted to investigate. Instead, reaching an awareness of the truth of those principles was *evidence* that one had reached correct philosophical— and, simultaneously, religious—understanding. It represented, for him, the highest goal of human activity: to know God.

Like many in the modern world, the medieval Jewish philosophers who struggled to reconcile science and religion were especially challenged by the biblical description of creation. Aristotelian science saw the world as eternal, with no beginning and no end. The idea that God, in an act of will, created the world from nothing seemed to fly in the face of rational understanding. In this debate Abravanel came down on the side of creation, insisting that the God of Israel is a God who constantly reveals himself in history, through miracles great and small. If the scientific viewpoint denied this, then it was wrong.

Abravanel was thoroughly engaged in the debates of the medieval philosophers. Although his stance was sometimes critical, he has been described as the last of the Jewish Aristotelians. As he left Spain for Naples in 1492 with his wife[1] and three sons, he moved from what had been the center of medieval European culture to what was becoming the birthplace of the Renaissance. His sons, who were young men when they accompanied their parents to Naples, blossomed in the intellectual and artistic climate of their new home. Abravanel had close relationships with his sons, and especially with his eldest, Judah (ca. 1465–1521), who became well known in his own right as an early Renaissance philosopher, poet, and physician. In Italy he was called "Leone Ebreo" (the Hebrew Lion), a nickname presumably drawn from the image of the Lion of Judah.

It was in Naples that the Abravanel family encountered Italian humanism. Influenced by the Greek and Latin classics, humanism valued the secular over the supernatural, worldly pleasure over monastic asceticism, and aesthetic beauty over scholastic precision—a sharp contrast with medieval monasticism. In Heschel's view, the humanistic way of thinking that Abravanel learned from his son, Leone Ebreo, influenced his own work profoundly, leading him, for example, to focus more than his predecessors on how the lower world influences the higher, not only on causation from above to below. Heschel must have enjoyed the way content and form came together in this educational moment: a son teaches a father to overturn the top-down hierarchy at the heart of medieval thought.

Abravanel wrote commentaries on nearly all the books of the Bible, and Heschel discusses his approach in the fifth section of this part, "Interpreting Scripture." Abravanel developed a new format:

he began his biblical commentaries with an introduction, explaining the historical and political context in which each biblical book was situated. In discussing the historical slant of Abravanel's biblical scholarship, Heschel makes the remarkable comment that he was "the true founder of *Wissenschaft des Judentums.*" This term refers to a movement that began in nineteenth-century German Jewish intellectual circles with a commitment to apply modern scholarly methods to the study of Judaism. Over the next century and a half, *Wissenschaft* learning became the basis of modernist Jewish studies, such as the examination of the Bible through the lenses of history and archeology. If Abravanel's methods were indeed similar to those of *Wissenschaft*, his interpretation of those methods was like that of Heschel himself: he used his historical and anthropological perspective not to debunk Jewish tradition, but to serve it.

In the final section, Heschel assesses Abravanel's life. He criticizes the messianism that "doomed" Abravanel's historical thinking, and he mourns what he calls a "shipwrecked life." But he also finds much to admire, and many of these admirable traits are reminiscent of Heschel himself: Abravanel was deeply loyal, both to his colleagues and to the Jewish people; though he lived in a time of religious persecution, "he respected Christianity and remained on friendly and loyal terms with Christians"; he saw "exalted meaning" in human existence; he lived in a balance between thinking and doing, contemplation and worldliness; and his faith did not depend on the outcome of theological grappling, rather, his interest in those struggles came from the conviction that engaging with the received tradition was invariably a meaningful and relevant project. Like Heschel, "Abravanel was mainly concerned about the future of Israel and of mankind."

On History

History is the encounter of the eternal and the temporal. As the word is a vessel for revelation and prayer, so history furnishes a receptacle for God's actions in the world and the material for the fulfillment of humanity through time.

Only rarely does the present shine a light that illuminates our understanding of the meaning of this encounter. But the past's truth concerns us always and everywhere, and sometimes that which is elusive when close to us will reveal itself from a distance.

God's Spirit speaks from the events of history, and our life is interconnected with this Spirit. Whenever our historical memory grows cloudy, the abandoned Spirit awakens in us, and we know again: we are servants of God's grace.

Our honor is given to us as a pledge for our loyalty to Israel. Human guilt and divine favor determine our being: through the single individual the entire people share in the guilt; through the entire people the individual shares in the favor.

The Jewish question is a question that God asks of us. Our existence is the history of a responsibility and the prehistory of a response.

The present is a reunion with the past. But the future will see again that which has never been seen before.

A Life between State and God

The Portuguese treasury was empty. King Afonso V, "the African," was determined to acquire the crown of Castile and to conquer the coastal cities of North Africa.[2]

Everybody dreamed of the fairy-tale riches of India. The Portuguese readied big ships for distant travels and possessed the best fleet of their time. The compass had been invented, adventurousness was in high gear, undreamed-of possibilities became a reality, and the desire for trade and material gain was greater than ever before. Portugal was close to becoming the mightiest naval and colonial power, and Lisbon the most important trade city in the world. Yet the king thought only of Castile and the coastal cities of North Africa and invested more and more in military activities. As a result, his treasury was depleted. Finances had to be regulated, loans had to be secured, further measures had to be taken.

It was to the solution of these difficult problems that Don Yitzhak Abravanel devoted himself.

Who was Don Yitzhak Abravanel? He was, in effect, the king's treasurer. His talent as well as his descent predestined him for this activity. He traced his family tree back to King David, and his father had been the treasurer of Prince Fernando, King Duarte's[3] brother. But we do not know when he started serving King Afonso. Ever since the beginning of the fifteenth century, members of the Abravanel family, who had emigrated from Castile, were among the most influential merchants and bankers of Lisbon; and they were not only the main importers of cloth from Flanders but also royal tax collectors and financiers. Born in Lisbon in 1437, Don Yitzhak acquainted himself early on with its noblemen and its economic and political realities. His wealth and his culture brought him respect and recognition. When, in 1480, the king needed 12 million *reales*, Don Yitzhak alone furnished more than one-tenth of that amount.

Young Abravanel, who apparently had been a disciple of the rabbi and exegete Judah Hayyun of Lisbon, was on friendly terms with scholars and sages, well versed in many areas of knowledge. He was at home in all fields of Jewish literature, in *halachah* and *aggadah*,[4] in religious philosophy and exegesis, and also in Christian theology and Islamic philosophy.

He knew Plato (like many other medieval scholars, he believed him to have been a student of Jeremiah[5]) and Aristotle, "*the* philosopher," Cicero and Seneca, Plotinus and Porphyrius, the commentators of Aristotle and the Latin historians. He was acquainted with Arabic thinkers (Alfarabi, Ibn Sina, Gazali, Averroes) and Christian thinkers (Jerome, Augustine, Albertus Magnus, Thomas of Aquino, Nicolas of Lyra).

His main interest, however, was the content of the Jewish faith and the interpretation of the Holy Scripture. In his youth he wrote an essay, "The Crown of the Elders," in which he discussed the concept of divine providence. He lectured on the philosophical teachings of Maimonides, whom he admired, although at times he declared, "This is the opinion of Rabbi Moses, but not that of our Teacher Moses."[6] In his character and thinking he was conservative, and the very title of his early work—"The Crown of the Elders"—confirms this attitude.

At the brilliant court of King Afonso he occupied an influential position. There he was well liked and honored. "I liked to live in the King's shadow, and I was close to him. He leaned on my arms," as he was to express it later on. Even more clearly: "I was happy at the palace of King Afonso, that mighty king, who ruled over vast countries situated on two seas, and was successful in all his enterprises. He occupied the throne of justice and saw to it that law and justice ruled everywhere. He trusted in God and respected Him, kept away from evil and sought his people's welfare. He was wise when the leaders of his people gathered, and no one equaled him as an instructor."[7]

He was on friendly terms with the nobles and particularly with the House of Braganza, an illegitimate offshoot of the royal family.

When 250 Jews were taken captive during the conquest of a Moroccan city, Abravanel initiated a collection of funds in order to redeem them. When one of his friends accompanied a Portuguese delegation to Rome, Abravanel asked him to intervene with the Pope in favor of the oppressed Jews. In the words of his son, he was "the Jews' shield and bulwark, saved the oppressed from the power of their enemies, healed their wounds and drove the wild lions away."[8]

Favored by providence, Abravanel lived a happy life in Lisbon. "I was happy in my homeland, well provided for by a paternal inheritance, in a home filled with blessings from above, in Lisbon, that famous capital of the kingdom of Portugal. There God blessed my abode. I had wealth and honor and the best that people had to offer. I built for myself houses and palaces, which were a meeting place for sages. Justice was meted out there, and books as well as scholars provided good judgment, understanding, and the fear of God. In my house and within my walls there were riches and charity, a memorial and a name, Torah scholarship and greatness, as with the heroes of times gone by."[9]

As a *moradore em Lisboa*—a resident of Lisbon—he was permitted to ride a mule and to go out without the Jewish emblem that had been prescribed by the so-called Afonsine code.[10] He also received property in Queluz.

However, the happy period was not to last long. King Afonso, a promoter of science and the arts, whose magnanimous gifts had earned him the friendship of the nobility, "had eaten from the Tree of Knowledge, but God did not want him to touch the Tree of Life, too."[11] He died in 1481, and his successor, his son João II, was, in politics and character, the opposite of his father.

It was the period in which the kings of Europe were trying to break the power of feudalism in order to establish the absolute power of the monarchy. The new king, who was in complete accord with this trend, thus set out on a path that was in direct opposition to his father's political values.

On December 15, 1481, he signed an edict in Evora, according to which all privileges granted by previous kings were to be examined. The nobles, having received great wealth from the deceased king, united in defense. The Duke of Braganza, a brother-in-law of the king and the most influential of the recipients—almost one-third of the entire acreage of the kingdom was his—conspired with King Ferdinand and Queen Isabella of Spain, since the nobles expected to be supported by them in their fight against the royal measures. When the Portuguese king was apprised of this move, he had the Duke of Braganza arrested on May 29, 1483, accused of treason, and executed. In the course of that year the same fate caught up with the Duke of Vizeu, a friend of Abravanel, and eighty members of the highest nobility.

Abravanel had indeed been on very friendly terms with the Duke of Braganza. But he denied that he had had any hand in the rebellion. In that argument he stood between the king and the noblemen. As far as his preferences were concerned, he leaned toward the latter. To him, King João was "a new King, lacking common sense. He had a change of heart, hated the noblemen and suspected his servants. In particular, he hated all his father's friends, the best among the nobility, who occupied the highest rank in the kingdom, and were known for their perfection and dignity. They were even relatives of his, bone of his bones, flesh of his flesh. He maliciously addressed them as follows: 'You have committed a capital crime, for all of you have conspired against me so as to deliver me and my country into the hands of the kings of Spain.' One of the most noble among them, second only to the king (he believed himself to be safe), was arrested and executed by the sword. His brothers fled for their lives to the mountains. They were terrified to see their pride fallen—their hero, the prince of their tribe, killed. Afraid for their lives, they vanished and were cut off—finished. The king took hold of all their possessions and destroyed the entire royal family.

"He was enraged even against me, although I had not sinned against him in deed or word. But in earlier, happier days I had been friendly with those noblemen who were now persecuted, and had given them the advice they had sought. The king accused me of grave crimes, he hated me mightily and counted me as one of the rebels. For, according to him, the latter would not have undertaken anything without informing me, as I was so closely allied with them. Thus I was considered a rebel like them. In addition, evil men, who tried to bring me down, whetted their tongues like serpents and accused me of evil deeds which I had neither committed nor even thought of."[12]

In the midst of this confusion Abravanel was summoned to the king in June 1483. Without any suspicion he obeyed. But while spending a night at an inn someone advised him: "Go no further—save your life, for these are bad times, evil rumors are circulating, everybody is afraid, and I hear that several people have conspired against you."

This information made him leave his homeland, his family, his wealth, and his rank. He left at night "in order to escape that evil master: misfortune." Since fate had hit him so suddenly, "like the whirlwind that scatters the chaff," he could not hold on to his possessions but saved his bare life.

When, on the following morning, his flight became known, the king had servants sent after him "to seize him and kill him at once." A great many of them were dispatched, and mercenaries on horseback pursued him all through the day and the following night.

"But divine grace prevented him" from being harmed. He reached Segura de la Orden in Castile safely. "When the king realized that he could not deprive me of my life he became enraged and treated me like an enemy. He took all my gold, silver, and jewelry. I had possessed more than anyone else in that country. He claimed whatever could be moved, without exception."[13] On May 30, 1485, Abravanel was condemned to death in absentia.

To Abravanel, Castile, the home of his ancestors, was no exile. He quickly made friends with the noblest Jews of Spain. His wife and sons, who were permitted to leave Portugal without him, also came to Castile.

He reacted to his harsh fate with equanimity. "It was good for me that I was humbled, so that I might learn Your laws. I prefer the teaching You proclaimed to thousands of gold and silver pieces" (Psalm 119:70–71).[14] His son, Leone Ebreo (Judah Abravanel), testified as follows: "Whatever the day brought—the dealings of the king, the troubles, the threat to his life—could not move him from the Torah and did not prevent him from reading in it day by day."[15]

Abravanel had complained that during the days that he had spent "in the royal palaces," dedicated to public activities, he had to neglect his studies.[16] While in Portugal, he could not complete his great commentary on the Bible.

During this initial stay in Spain, he seems to have devoted himself mainly to intellectual work. Freed from the business of finances and of the State, he pursued biblical studies. In a surprisingly short time he wrote his commentary on the books of Joshua and Samuel.

But the solitude of the scholarly way of life was not in harmony with his character. His life was torn between political and theological activity. When, in Portugal, he had advised King Afonso V in financial matters, he complained that matters of the State had caused him to neglect his intellectual work. In Castile, he initially found leisure for writing. But soon he served the Spanish kings and again gave up his research. It is hard to say what, in his heart of hearts, he would rather have been, a statesman or a theologian. He was apparently attracted by both the will to act and the love of contemplation.

Leone Ebreo enthusiastically described his father's fame as a statesman: "Great in counsel, great in rulership and honor, his heart as broad as the sand spewed up by the seas. Kings, lords and generals ask every day for his advice. In every branch of science, in wisdom and intelligence, his ideas accommodate every wish."[17]

Later Abravanel related: "At the very moment that I wished to begin my commentary on the book of Kings, I was called to the mightiest among the princes, the king of Spain, who ruled over Castile, Aragon, Catalonia, Sicily, and other islands. I came to the court of the king and the queen. And by divine grace I found favor in their eyes and those of the noblemen, who occupied the highest seats in the council."[18] The year was 1484.

Together with other reports, this call leads to the conclusion that Abravanel not only conducted an extensive financial business but also held an important position in the State, comparable to a Secretary of the Treasury. The main concern of Spanish politics at that time was to destroy the last traces of Islamic rule on the Iberian

Peninsula. For many years there had been a war against Granada, which was ruled by the Moors. This was extremely expensive. In order to continue that war, all economic power in the country had to be put to work.

Abravanel served a royal court in which the Grand Inquisitor Torquemada, the queen's father confessor, provoked hatred of the Jews. It was there that the project of exterminating Jewry was forged. The tragedy of Abravanel's brilliant career was nowhere more evident than here. His experience and talents were put to use toward an undertaking that would prove to be catastrophic for Spanish Jewry.

On January 2, 1492, the Spanish kings entered Granada. On March 31, 1492, a decree was issued at the Alhambra, according to which all Jews were to be expelled from their Spanish homeland.

How did Abravanel react in that terrible hour?

"At that time I was at the royal court and exhausted myself in petitions. Three times I begged of him: 'Help, O King, why do you want to act thus against your servants? Let us rather redeem our lives with gold and silver—whatever an Israelite possesses he will give for his homeland.' I turned to my friends who stood in good graces with the king, that they might intervene for the sake of my people. The noblest among them did speak fervently to the king, that he might recall those angry decrees and give up his plan to destroy the Jews. But he neither listened nor replied. The queen very eloquently supported him and encouraged him to bring his initial project to fruition.

"Thus were our efforts without success. I had neither

peace nor rest, and yet the disaster hit us. The people in whose midst I lived left the country, three hundred thousand on foot, the young and the old, women and children, on one and the same day. Wherever the Spirit induced them to go, there they went, and their King— God—led them. One of them called out, 'I belong to God,' and another one devoted his strength to the Lord. Some of them went to nearby Portugal or Navarra, but bitter sufferings and great disaster were their fate everywhere—rapaciousness, famine, and pestilence. Some went to the ocean and sought for themselves a path in its waves."[19]

Abravanel could not go to Portugal, where many Jews had tried to find a refuge. With other emigrants he went with his children to Naples.

At that time Ferrante I of Aragon ruled over Naples, and he offered hospitality to the victims of the Spanish king. Many foreigners there had attained great power and honor, and Abravanel was soon regarded highly. Abravanel's possessions in Spain had been largely confiscated by the government, which mitigated for him and his family the prohibitions against exports that were decreed against other emigrants.[20] Thus he did not arrive in Naples as a pauper, and in addition the king gave him an important financial position.

Abravanel was now in Italy, the country of the Renaissance and of humanism. His son, later to become famous as Leone Ebreo, was thirty years old when he entered Italy, a contemporary of Leonardo and Bramante. Here he experienced something entirely new: the idea of beauty. But for Abravanel, who, at the age of fifty-six, was all too familiar with life's vicissitudes, the encounter with the Italian Renaissance was of no great importance. In Naples, where there were more humanists in high positions than in any other state but Florence, Abravanel worked side by side with the famous Pontano, secretary to the king.[21]

In Portugal Abravanel had been just one of the victims of a general political crisis; in Spain, he had become one of the targets of Jewish fate. Now, having immigrated to Naples, he became involved in the downfall of the Aragonese royalty, for Ferrante I had to defend his throne against the claims of the kings of France. Without a national kingdom and having only a few weak-kneed friends to support him, he succeeded in establishing his rule only after a long struggle against the local allies of the House of Anjou and the mighty Neapolitan barons. But in the end he succeeded.[22] He was a very active, humanistically educated prince, and famous for his generous gifts. His methods are known to us through Machiavelli's book *The Prince*. When he died, on May 25, 1494, his son Alfonso II ascended to the throne, but he immediately abdicated in favor of his son and left for Messina, accompanied by Abravanel, who remained there until the king's death, November 19, 1495.

In the meantime, a rebellion broke out in Naples in February 1495 and the people, having been incited by the authorities, robbed the Jews of their possessions. While Abravanel remained loyal to the king and accompanied him to Sicily, his precious library, and whatever else he owned in Naples, were stolen or destroyed.

Abravanel, who again experienced "want instead of

wealth,"[23] went to the island of Corfu, which, like the other Greek islands, was at that time a subject of the Venetian Republic. The Jews, whose economic importance had been appreciated by the republic, acquired civil rights and enjoyed safety and peace. Here, Abravanel began his commentary on the book of Isaiah.

In 1496 he returned to the kingdom of Naples, which had meanwhile been conquered by the French. He settled at Nonopoli in Apulia, where he finished his commentary on Deuteronomy (already begun in Portugal). He also began his commentary on the Passover Haggadah and the *Sayings of the Fathers.*

He apparently kept up his relationship with the Neapolitan king, who wrote this letter of recommendation for him and his son: "Because of their capabilities, we greatly treasure our dear Don Yitzhak Abravanel and his son, the physician Leone, and wish them to settle, together with their family, in our city of Naples, in order to serve us."[24]

In 1503 the Kingdom of Naples came under the rule of the Spanish kings. This may have been the reason for Abravanel's moving that year to Venice, where his son Joseph had already taken abode. Once again the indefatigable man—by now sixty-six—conceived a great plan and undertook an ambitious political action.

In 1499 Vasco da Gama had returned to Lisbon after having sailed around the Cape of Good Hope and discovered the sea route to India. Ever since that time the economic supremacy of the Venetian Republic had begun to decline. There developed a vast difference in price between those wares imported to Portugal via the cheap sea route around Africa and those that had taken the more expensive land route over Egypt and the Near East. "In 1503 the pepper sold in Venice cost five times as much as that sold in Lisbon." People everywhere spoke of the dangers Venice faced because of Portuguese navigation.

The Venetians themselves did not take the Portuguese enterprise too seriously and tried initially to conclude a treaty with the sultan and the Indian princes. Then, between 1502 and 1504, they considered building a canal between the Red Sea and the Mediterranean. They never considered coming to terms with Portugal.

After the expulsion of the Jews from Spain, Abravanel still remained in touch with King Fernando, and when the Spanish king visited Naples, Leone Ebreo even joined in his retinue. Abravanel also maintained his connections with Portugal, especially since João II had died, and the new ruler, Emanuel, was a brother of the Duke of Vizeu, a friend of Abravanel's. These relationships were so influential that Abravanel could propose to the Senate of Venice the negotiation of a trade treaty concerning spices with Portugal. The Council of Ten[25] accepted his offer, and Abravanel declared himself willing to send his nephew to Lisbon as his agent.

Even during his lifetime, Abravanel acquired fame as a theologian and a philosopher, and equally as a statesman. "Sages rise in his presence and rush to listen to him, as hinds rush to water. They wait for his words as one would for rain, and they rush to hear him, as dew drops on grass. They open their mouths wide to receive the honey of his lessons."[26]

Saul ha-Cohen of Crete, a disciple of Elijah del Medigo,

addressed a number of philosophical questions to him, which, along with the answers, have come down to us.[27]

He prepared for publication *Nahalat Avot,* a commentary on the *Sayings of the Fathers*; *Zaveh Pesach,* a commentary on the Passover Haggadah, and *Rosh Amanah,* a tractate concerning the principles of the faith.

His son Leone visited him in 1505 and wrote a dedicatory poem to each of these works. They appeared that same year, published in Constantinople by the Brothers Nehemias.

He died January 13, 1509, in Venice, the city whose supremacy he had tried to save. He was buried in Padua.

"In him were united greatness, wealth and wisdom, the merits of the fathers and a zeal for God. His nobility, his piety, and his straightforwardness were greater than can be expressed by word."[28]

On the Origin of the World

The realm of problems in which Abravanel's thought moved was determined not so much by his own concerns as by the trends of contemporary Jewish philosophy. At the time, the thirteen dogmas stipulated by Maimonides were at the center of the discussion. But how philosophy's themes had changed! What mattered was no longer the reshaping of *faith into knowledge* but the protecting of *faith against heresy*. For Maimonides the dogmas had been the minimum requisite of a philosophical knowledge of God; for the fifteenth-century religious philosophers they were the condition for correct faith. The breaking away from the teachings of Maimonides was also evident in content—in the reduction of the number of dogmas that followed from Crescas and Albo.

Abravanel himself was deeply imbued with a belief in the equal value of all teachings and phrases in the Holy Scripture and of the obligations they entail. The sentences "The sons of Cham were Kush and Mitzraim" (1 Chronicles 1:8) and "I am the Lord, your God, who brought you forth from the land of Egypt" (Exodus 20:2) carry the same authority. He believed that there is no place in doctrine for dogmas that are drawn up like scientific axioms—religion and science are too different. But Abravanel, whose relationship to Maimonides does not fit entirely into the succession of the Maimonideans nor the frontline of the anti-Maimonideans, heard internally the exhortation that Maimonides's "spirit and soul" directed to him: to defend his teaching against the attacks of Crescas and Albo.[29] This motive for writing about the problem of dogma in *Rosh Amanah* (Principle of Faith) is also typical of his other writings.

Abravanel rejected philosophical rationalism and subscribed instead to a supranaturalistic worldview that reminds us in some ways of Judah Halevi.[30] "In the Torah of Moses there is neither speculative philosophy nor are there logical investigations, for to attain a bliss that is beyond the intellect and beyond nature only faith and good deeds are necessary."[31] The *direct communion with God*, the greatest of all miracles, arises not through philosophical speculation but through divine grace. Humans, limited as they are, engage in speculation, but they come to communion with God from a position that is beyond humanness. As a human being, a Jew is destined to be formed intellectually; as a Jew, he is destined to attain direct communion with God. Thus the Jew is subordinate to no intermediary, but to God alone. For God dwells with Israel, and providence is an unmediated expression of this indwelling, the Shechina.[32]

The question of the origin of the world concerned Abravanel more than all other philosophical questions, and in *The Works of God* it became the object of a penetrating and comprehensive investigation. His only larger systematic work, it stems from the insight that faith in the creation of the world is "a foundation of Torah," a foundation whose origin lies neither in Moses's thought nor in any ancient human tradition, but rather in divine revelation.[33]

In their encounter with Greek philosophy, the theologians of Judaism, Christianity, and Islam strove to find common ground among their ideas. But however much

the parallels actually or apparently enabled convergen-
ces, so the divergences, too, became equally evident.
The incompatibility was clearly shown by the question
of *the origin of the world*. The rationalistic thinking of
Aristotelianism, whose epistemological aim was to
understand the universe as a system of airtight necessity,
asserts—in contrast to the biblical account of creation—
that the world is *eternal*. There was no lack of attempts to
prove the creation of the world by means of reason, but
Maimonides (1138–1204) was able to challenge the Aristotelian position with philosophical arguments, while also
denying the possibility of answering this question ratio-
nally. He came down on the side of faith. Nonetheless,
he did not succeed in closing off the discussion, which
was then reopened by his successors Gersonides (1288–
1344) and Crescas (1340–1410). The kernel of this lively
discussion is that the answer to the question of the origin
of the world is not only a superstructure of theoretical
knowledge but also the fundamental teaching of doctrine.
Maimonides sees the actual contradiction between the
assertion that the world is eternal and the Jewish teaching not in the denial of a temporal beginning but in the
corresponding view that the world *necessarily* follows
from God and is dependent on God's existence, "like the
effect from its cause,"[34] like the ray of light from the sun,
so that God can alter nothing about the course of the natural order. "He cannot lengthen the wing of any fly, nor
shorten the foot of any ant."[35] But the consequence is to
deny both the miracles that our ancestors saw with their
own eyes, as well as reward and punishment—which,
after all, do not result from the natural order of things.[36]

Maimonides had refrained from untying this Gordian knot. Nissim of Gerona[37] and his student Crescas, on the other hand, attempted to reconcile the concept of the eternity of the world with Jewish doctrine: the world is not—in contrast to the Aristotelian understanding—a necessary consequence of the divine being but rather a product of the free divine will, and since God's will is eternal, so, too, is this, its product. Even if this position were rejected because the temporal creation of the world is explicitly attested to in the Bible, the teaching of the creation need not be regarded as a fundamental article of faith, as dogma, for the acceptance of the idea of the eternity of the world can be seen as consistent with religious teachings. Scripture, after all, includes no commandment like "Hear, O Israel, the world has been created."[38]

Abravanel sharply rejects as self-contradictory this attempt to understand the world as an eternally existing product of God's will. For only the existence of that which was once possible and nonexistent can be seen as the effect of divine will. On the other hand, that which has always existed is a necessity, independent in its existence, something that cannot be viewed as a consequence of God's will. And then miracles, God's intervention in the course of nature, would also be an impossibility, for if the world as a whole in its natural order is of eternal permanence, so then must be its parts. Indeed, we are no more commanded to believe in the temporal creation of the world than we are in God's oneness. For the commandments are related only to action, not to beliefs. "Hear, O Israel" is not a commandment to believe in the teaching of God's oneness, but an exhortation "to hear the teaching and to study it" in order to attain thereby the love for God and perfect faith.

The same holds true for the belief in creation. It is attained by practical means: by keeping the holiness of the Sabbath, which was instituted to remember the creation of the world.[39]

Abravanel also had to defend the idea of creation from another side. Deviating from Maimonides, Gersonides— who joins Maimonides in disputing the idea of the non-creation of the world—sees the temporal beginning of the world, but not the creation out of nothing, as the essential element in the doctrine of creation. He teaches the theory of the creation of the world out of *primal matter*, a theory that goes back to the Platonic dialogue Timaeus.[40]

Abravanel refutes this rejection of the concept of creation ex nihilo, which Maimonides and Judah Halevi[41] had declared as religiously acceptable, with philosophical and religious arguments.[42] Faith does not demand that something that contradicts reason be held as true. But this often-expressed claim has to be deemed incorrect— that since nothing can come out of nothing, creation ex nihilo is an impossibility, like, for example, the concept of a square whose diagonals are equal to its sides. We have to be able to differentiate between that which is absolutely impossible (when subject and predicate are irreconcilable, e.g., being is not being) and the relatively impossible (something the imagination cannot conceive of, e.g., a person who flies). The idea that the world came forth out of nothing would seem to be an example of the first, but the teaching of creation asserts that *God* created the world out of nothing.[43]

In a comprehensive critique of the philosophical discussion about the origin of the world,[44] Abravanel ultimately acknowledges the logic of the arguments for the world's eternity and the ineffectiveness of the counterarguments.[45] For that reason he refrains from basing the doctrine of creation on speculation. "I examine my paths and return home to the tradition of the ancients, in which God resides. I choose the path of faith. I hate doubt and speculation. Musing on the inconceivable is idle. In order to separate the holy from the profane, the pure from the impure, I will convey my opinion about that to you in a separate chapter."[46]

Thus Abravanel decides for tradition and against philosophy. The circle of Jewish philosophy of the Middle Ages closes—at its tail end—with a declaration of the primacy of tradition.

The Two Paths to the Imitation of God

Abravanel summarized his view in four principles:

1. God created the world of His own free will. As an act of free will, creation differs from a natural event in that it happens consciously. Further, natural events have consequences that are of one kind, e.g., fire warms but does not cool. An act of will, on the other hand, can have consequences that are opposed to one another.[47]

2. God is not only the creator of the world, He is its preserver. Without the sustaining effect of God's actions, the world would not continue, for as little as a thing can create itself, so little can it continue to sustain itself. The concept of nature, i.e., a fixed order, does not adequately explain the continuing existence of the world. Nature depends on the divine will that works in it.

3. The world is transitory.[48] Its existence is finite. It was created out of absolute nothingness and it will return to absolute nothingness. Before this world was created, countless worlds existed that were created and then disappeared. Nothing eternal exists except God, not even matter.[49]

4. The creation and the destruction of the world have a purpose. The one who acts sees the purpose of his action differently from those for whom the action was undertaken. For the builder, the purpose of building is his payment; for the owner, it is to live in the building. It is senseless to ask what purpose God intended in creating the world, for He, the

absolutely Perfect One, lacks nothing and sought nothing in creation. But what do God's creations see as the purpose of the world?

With our limited powers of understanding we intuit that the meaning of God's *thinking* is that he acknowledges himself, the perfect object of thought; of God's *acting*, that he gives things existence, endurance, and value, whereby they become capable of attaining a *resemblance with God*, commensurate with their level of being. The resemblance is manifested when things recognize God—that same object of thought—and then imbue the level of being below them with value. The unity of the cosmos, determined by the oneness of God, and the cohesion of all its parts are based on this resemblance. All of reality forms a hierarchy of beings, whose emanations stream forth from top to bottom, from the spiritual beings through the astral bodies down into the region of the elements, the lowest region of being. Everything that happens in nature is a cycle of purposes. On the lowest level of being, things begin their striving upward, "for, without question, the elements are there to create the hybrid form of composite things like minerals and metals." Plant forms strive toward the forms of living beings, and the forms of living beings strive toward the forms of rational beings that are characteristic of humans. The purpose of all these beings is the perfected human being, whose soul lives in community with God. In this sense, humans are the purpose of this lower world, insofar as they contain God's perfection and convey goodness and love to the other beings by their actions and according to their powers. For that is the meaning of the divine commandments. The ultimate purpose of all beings is community with God. For the purpose of all beings in the cycle of purposes is to attain resemblance with God: through knowledge of God and the outpouring of goodness and love.[50]

The world's transitoriness is determined by this purpose. For through the insight into their transitoriness, God's creations understand "that in their being they depend on God's will, that their existence is not necessary and that it issued forth from absolute nonbeing through God's goodness."[51]

Maimonides rejected the idea that the world had been created for a specific purpose, such as for the sake of humans, with the argument that the astral beings, who stand on a higher level than humans, cannot possibly have their purpose in humans.[52] For Abravanel, by contrast, it is precisely the activity of higher beings toward lower ones that is the means to the end of attaining resemblance to God, the necessary precondition for reaching the stage of perfection.

Behind this worldview one can sense a slight glimmer of the *Renaissance*, which was arising in the West at that time. While medieval thought was defined by a dualism of above and below, by a vertical hierarchy in which there was only a descent—from God to the lowest level of matter—now, coming out of classical traditions, there arose the awareness of the raising up of that which was below: the individual. Being is no longer felt as vertical, like a process in which the infinite flows into the finite, but rather like a cycle: the infinite, the spirit that flows from above to below into matter, flows upward again. The ascent follows upon the descent. That humans are "the end and the pinnacle of all sensate creatures, through whom the remanation of things into God takes place" is something that Nicholas of Cusa[53] (1401–64), whose writing Abravanel can hardly have known, also teaches.

More important than these parallels is the relationship between the teachings of Yitzhak Abravanel and the philosophy of his son, a relationship to which no attention has been paid until now. For Leone Ebreo, too, there exists "a cycle of the universe, whose beginning is the divinity, and from it follows in sequence, one linked to the next, the first matter, what is most distant from divinity, and from that another ascent follows, getting closer step by step, until it ends at the point from which it began."[54] "In the first semicircle, being descends in the manner of a creative emanation from the First Being— from the greater to the lesser to the lowest chaos, or rather to the first matter—and in the other semicircle, it ascends back from the lesser to the higher, like a return to that from which it first emanated."[55] "By its nature, the first matter desires and strives for the forms of the elements; the forms of the elements desire and strive for the mixed and vegetative forms; the vegetative forms, for the sensory forms; and the sensory forms love, with sensory love, the rational form."[56]

Leone, too, devotes a thorough examination to the question of the world's origin. He presents the Aristotelian, Platonic, and biblical conceptions and, like his father, admits that, by the laws of nature, nothing can come out of nothing, but that "miraculously, things can come out of nothing through God's omnipotence."[57] For him, too, God is not only the creator, but the preserver of the world. The world, however—and not just the things in it—is transitory. Upon its destruction, the creation of another world will follow.[58]

On the End of Time

The messianic promise of the prophets had predicted a harried but not utterly weakened people. In the souls of the exiled, the dark experience of the present mixed with the hope for the future—the expectation and the knowledge that the road of exile would lead to the end of times, the Great Hour when suffering will be proven to have been the birth pangs of redemption. How else was one to explain God's mercy, the Father's love?

Ever since 1464, misfortune had befallen the Jews more than ever before. No other people had gone through so much suffering. Jews had been exiled from Germany, Lombardy, Sicily, Sardinia, Russia, Castile, Lyon, Aragon, Catalonia, and Granada. From Spain alone, three hundred thousand Jews had emigrated.[59]

Along the coast of the Mediterranean, no miracle occurred. In 1497, the disaster crossed the borders of Portugal; from there, too, Jews were expelled. Everybody asked: Why does the son of Jesse not come? Which powers prevent his appearance? Will he never come?[60] What could be more urgent than a reply to such a question?

And yet, what could be more difficult? The Jewish belief in a Messiah was attacked from all sides. The Church "invited" the Jews to take part in public disputations, when Christian theologians tried to prove exegetically that the messianic promises of the prophets referred to Jesus, and had already been fulfilled.

It was not only the Christians who attacked the messianic dogma.

Jewish philosophers, too, disagreed with Maimonides,

stating that this belief was not of fundamental importance.[61] In addition, some Jewish exegetes staged an
ambush,[62] positing the theory that the Prophets' promises
had been fulfilled in the establishment of the Second
Commonwealth and Temple, which meant that messianic expectations were based on oral tradition, not
on the Bible. When the ancient faith came under this
heavy attack, disappointment broke the backbone of
the faithful. Their disillusionment approached despair.

In that hour of crisis, Abravanel wielded his authority, his scholarship, and his faith. Maimonides had at
one time faced the same dilemma. When the Jews of
Yemen approached him to rebut the false teachings of
pseudo-messianism, he spoke with intellectual simplicity,
personal warmth, and directness. But Abravanel had
neither the passion nor the power to talk to people in
familiar terms. His was not a statement addressed to the
people, but a trilogy addressed to scholars.[63] His was not
the role of an admonishing comforter and herald, but the
stance of a scholar and exegete. With typical exactitude
and detailed analysis, he approached the solution to
the problem. Thus he became the *theoretician* of *Jewish
messianic teaching*.

Abravanel himself was seized by messianic expectation. To him, the fundamental prophetic statement was:
"Before she travailed she gave birth" (Isaiah 66:7). Its
interpretation: Before she has pain, the savior will be
born. He explained: Before the sufferings of redemption
commence, the Redeemer will have been born. He was
convinced that the birth of the Anointed One had already
taken place, that he was born before the expulsion of

the Jews from Spain, just as Moses had been born at the beginning of great suffering.[64] He stated four basic principles: the messianic promise had not yet been fulfilled; the Messiah had already been born; he is a human being; he will not abolish the law.[65] This strengthened those who retained hope, who rejected some Jewish exegetes and the Christological interpretation. A careful analysis of the numerous biblical and talmudic statements conveyed to him the knowledge people had concerning the essence and the form of the messianic event, and these are his conclusions:

The Messianic Age will bring about the punishment of the pagan nations, the ingathering of the scattered Jews (including the ten lost tribes), the renewal of the spirit of prophecy, the participation of the entire people in knowledge and wisdom, the repentance of the apostates and of those forcibly intermixed with other nations, the crowning of a king of the Davidic dynasty, the precluding of future exile of the Jews, the recognition by all nations of the one God and His teaching, and eternal peace.

Redemption will mean the perfection of the human race. Human nature will be re-formed; men will not strive after physical desire, but after perfection.[66] Mankind will resemble Adam before the fall,[67] and in its entirety will be subject to immediate divine providence.[68] Since none of these promises were fulfilled after the rebuilding of the Second Temple, to attribute them to that period is error and falsification.[69]

Again and again, their attempt to guess the time of the messianic arrival misled the "reckoners of the end." Their speculations were based on the idea that the messianic kingdom would necessarily follow the same course as certain periods of world history. These periods of the kingdoms and their durations were indicated, it was thought, in the predictions of the prophets. The Talmud berated these reckoners, and history proved them wrong, but believers and the pious have repeatedly succumbed to the temptation.

Ideas of this kind are completely foreign to prophetic eschatology. The promised messianic kingdom is determined by God's will, not by some plan or the passing of a certain number of years. "Chiliastic"[70] ideas found their way into Judaism without ever attaining the status of legitimacy. In both Judaism and Christianity the assumption that the Scripture harbors signs of the future allowed for the development of an interpretative technique—aided by the methods of astrology—that based the prototype of all apocalypses on the prophetic books, and especially on the book of Daniel.

When "the end" is calculated it isn't the immediate experience of God, but rather a number, a formula that governs the thinking. What results is not revelation but myth, not a direct understanding of God, but arid interpretation of Scripture and history.

Abravanel, who was strongly attracted to apocalyptic thinking, succumbed to this temptation: he predicted that the Messiah would come in the year 1532. The eschatological calculations at that time were confirmations rather than determinations. But the theoretical justifications that Abravanel provided, especially those that derived from stellar constellations, were a decline into mythological thinking.

The error had a soothing effect, but it also prepared a false path. In 1502, in Asturia near Venice, there appeared Asher Lämmlin,[71] who purported to be the herald of the Anointed One and found numerous followers among Jews and Christians.

Interpreting Scripture

By looking at the paths that lead Jews to the words of Scripture, we can identify both the level and the particular condition of the Jewish mind of the times. Various crises and many different attitudes toward faith bring people to the literal meaning or cause them to speculate about the deeper meaning. The degree of immediacy in the former as well as the amount of artfulness in the latter differ in their methods and their imagined aims. Abravanel strikes a new chord in the rich register of scriptural interpretation that was available in the fifteenth century. He is the first to have introduced the historical method into biblical exegesis.

The significance of this step was revolutionary. To the Middle Ages the Bible appears against the background of eternity. The individual encounters it as the word behind which he discerns and hears God's voice. Of its content he knows only that it is sacred. The historical reality that the word reports barely stirs his curiosity. Its eternal validity shines brighter than its embodied content.

In Abravanel a historical view was awakened. He was Judaism's first *humanist*. He was interested not only in the biblical text but in the biblical age. His faith in the same source of revelation for all biblical books was unshakable, but he also had a sure sense of their stylistic and structural differences. His unshakeable respect for the text, which determined his thinking and being unequivocally, was united with a naive daring that allowed him to look closely into questions of history.

Abravanel is the true founder of *Wissenschaft des Judentums*, even if he had little influence on its development. His combination of encyclopedic knowledge with a universal understanding of life, his sense of factuality and clarity of judgment became extremely fruitful for his research. But it was precisely this versatility that was harmful to his work. Both the particular themes of his own learning and traditional lines of inquiry were combined in his understanding.

The variety, disparity, and unevenness of the latter continually undermined the unity of his interpretation and robbed it of its ultimate consistency.

His language lacks a personal style. In his presentation he oriented himself to Jewish and non-Jewish models. In his Bible commentaries he proceeded with scholastic precision and elaborateness. To the text under discussion he added chains of questions, and formulated important and less important difficulties in the passage that he or his predecessors had noticed. Existing solutions were proven, disproven, or shown to be inadequate. Finally, his own conception was presented, whereby all the difficulties were solved in sequence. This method of presentation corresponded to the taste of the time. But this formalism, the long-windedness of his style, and the lack of methodological exclusivity are partly responsible for Abravanel's work finding neither recognition nor appropriate influence.

He, himself, was aware that in his interpretations of both the Bible and *aggadah* [72] he had gone beyond his predecessors.

Rashi[73] usually limited himself to repeating midrashic

interpretations of the Bible, Abraham Ibn Ezra [74] to establishing the grammatical form and lexical meanings. The other interpreters offer either homiletic interpretations or, likewise, only lexical commentaries.[75] Furthermore, the doubts alluded to by one exegete are ignored by the others.[76]

Abravanel's aim was to establish the straightforward meaning of the words, sharply rejecting allegorical exegeses, and even rejecting aggadic commentaries if they didn't agree with that straightforward meaning.

His interest in biblical archaeology could find little precedent in the works of the Jewish exegetes, who were largely focused either on philological questions of lexical forms or allegorical questions of inner meanings. By means of comparisons he tried to develop a feel for the conditions of biblical times. His insight into political, social, and economic issues and his strong sense for the real facts of this world stood him in good stead. Now and then he tried to understand as natural events those supernatural occurrences that the Bible depicts.

The Christian Bible interpreters of the seventeenth and eighteenth centuries (Buxtorf the Younger, Buddeus, Carpzow, et al.) studied Abravanel's commentaries and translated them into Latin. On the Jewish side, he influenced Moshe Alshech (sixteenth century) and M. L. Malbin (nineteenth century).

A Legacy of Failed Advocacy

Abravanel was not the herald of new ideas, but, rather, the trustee of right belief. He was not possessed by a philosophical *eros*. The teachings of revelation were to him an answer, not a problem.

His strongest human quality, growing out of both his spiritual approach and his entire style of life, was *loyalty*—in his life and in his teaching, at royal courts and in the House of Learning, inwardly and outwardly—in each of these areas, if need be to death.

We need not emphasize the fact that Abravanel did not commit treason when, in 1492, the year of the expulsion of the Jews from Spain, he and his family had to choose between baptism and exile.[77] That situation, in which he proved himself so firm, gained a special meaning through the opposite decision of his friend Abraham Señor, who accepted baptism.

Loyalty, which the Jewish dignitaries of that century had lost, formed Abravanel's very soul. The injuries to which his life had been exposed and the disaster that befell his people could not weaken him. The *firmness* of his being, which distinguished him in an age of catastrophes, is remarkable. In his view, not Jeremiah, but Isaiah and Ezekiel, are the models for Israel to follow.[78] The same held true for him. In the expulsion from Spain he saw the greatest disaster the Jews had suffered since the destruction of the Temple; but he stood under the banner of Isaiah's promise, not Jeremiah's lamentations.

Unlike some of his contemporaries, who lived through the collapse of Spanish-Jewish civilization, he did not resent philosophy and secular science. Even in his apologetics he respected Christianity and remained on friendly and loyal terms with Christians.[79]

His life was essentially filled by the exalted meaning that he saw in the existence of man in general. In this existence, these are the two paths within the Imitation of God.

He represented a harmony between the two paths: the *vita activa* and the *vita contemplativa*. This harmony did not survive in Judaism. Even his son wrote: "The human soul, which is basically *one*, distances itself from the *vita contemplativa* when devoting itself to the *vita activa*; but when it dedicates itself to contemplation, it considers the business of this world as nothing."[80] "My spirit, disgusted with the doings of this world and the need for such base activity, withdraws into itself."[81]

Such is the mood of the generation of the exiled. The best sons of Spanish Jewry emigrated to the Holy Land, where they devoted themselves to the contemplations of Jewish mysticism; and pessimism never disappeared from the blood of Sephardic Jewry, which had once loved this world so much.

What is strange about this unique occurrence is its *historicity*. And in many aspects: as *life*, as *a way of thought*, as *a spiritual encounter* and as *goal*.

Abravanel was driven by the historical aim of collaborating with the drama of the political, social, and economic powers. He, the theologian, did not see a conflict, not even a problem, in his political activity. He acted naturally, feeling that this was in accord with his being. It was easy for him to adapt himself again and again to new political and economic situations. His share in the doings of this world has its source in his own soul. His thinking, too, was determined by a historical drive. In interpreting the Bible—his main concern—he was as much interested in historical facts as in explaining the text. To a medieval scholar, questions concerning the author and the life as presented in Holy Writ were rather rare. To Abravanel, they were the expression of an intensively historical orientation.[82]

In his theological writings he dealt with cosmological and theological questions not because he had confronted these problems himself and had had to wrestle with them personally. They were questions passed on to him, primarily as the ideas of earlier thinkers. He was engaging with the historical tradition, not struggling with and resolving a personal crisis.

To him, tradition, and not his private feelings, was the decisive source. He never voluntarily dealt with Jewish dogmatics. Ironically, though, he came back to them again and again, but only polemically, when a theme of historic interest had to be treated.

Unlike Maimonides, who was interested in the eternal salvation of the individual, Abravanel was mainly concerned about the future of Israel and of mankind. The central interest of his mind was the messianic kingdom, which he expected in the near future, and in this world. What moved him most was not mystical beatitude within God, or within an active intellect emanating from Him, but the historical reformation of mankind.

His historical thinking was doomed. His messianism ended in chiliasm. His historical way of thinking, the consequence of which could have attained important meaning in his commentaries, had almost no effect. After him, biblical investigation was exchanged for talmudic investigation, and Abravanel's exegesis had neither influence nor echo.

Occupation with the Bible became divine service. Scholars did not want to satisfy their intellect with grammatical or historical knowledge, but to calm their souls with the sanctifying waters of the biblical word.

Abravanel's life was a rock formed, pulverized, and moved by the winds. He supported a king who was to destroy the Jews. He served states from which he had to flee. He amassed wealth that was confiscated.

His most important historical moment arrived when he appeared before King Ferdinand, offering a large sum of money in return for annulment of the decree of expulsion. He was unsuccessful. But what people remember best about Abravanel's statesmanlike activity, and about him generally, is this vain effort.

It was meaningful. It justified his standing in the center of that tragic happening. His personal fate mirrored the national one. He appeared to be the symbol of a tragic epoch; but equally meaningful and justified was the fame of his failed petition.

The fragility of man and his works is visible in the area of history as well as in physiology. Even if a man be a governmental minister, history deprives him of his independence, although for a limited time he appears independent.

This shipwrecked life is a symbol of the last act of Jewish history in Europe. For a long time after the Jews were expelled from Spain they played no active diplomatic role in Europe.

The last rays of autumn flickered around the person of Abravanel, that last remainder of a brilliant epoch. Never again do we find a similar figure combining Torah and worldly greatness. When the last Spanish Jew left his homeland, Sephardic Jewry fell into agony.

The Jews, who had held imposing positions in the state, in economy and in society, left their Spanish homeland. The conquest of the New World was accomplished without their collaboration. Had they remained on the Iberian Peninsula, they most probably would have taken part in the enterprises of the conquistadores. When the latter arrived on Haiti, they found over one million inhabitants. Twenty years later one thousand remained.

The desperate Jews of 1492 could not know that a favor had been done them.

PART 4

For the Jewish Holidays in Berlin

Context

Heschel occasionally used his column in the *Gemeindeblatt* to prepare his audience for upcoming Jewish holidays. For example, on April 5, 1936, the paper published his detailed set of instructions for conducting the Passover seder. Two of the *Gemeindeblatt* items that follow—"The Power of Repentance" and "The Meaning of Repentance"—were offered in preparation for Rosh Hashanah in September 1936. The third, "Lights over the Sea," was written for Hanukkah in November 1937.

The first Rosh Hashanah piece appeared in the regular installment of the *Gemeindeblatt* on Sunday, September 13, the Sunday before Rosh Hashanah. The second ran on Wednesday, September 16, the eve of the holiday. A theme word in both essays is, in German, *Umkehr*, which Heschel has used to translate the Hebrew *teshuvah* and which we have rendered into English as "repentance." It must be noted that there is a richness to the German and Hebrew terms that cannot be completely expressed by any single word in English. *Teshuvah,* which comes from the root *shuv,* meaning "to return," can refer to either the spiritual "return" of repentance or a more literal return—coming back to a place of origin or to a former status. It is also the Hebrew word for a response, an answer. Similarly, The German *Umkehr* means both repentance and a literal turning back. In the context of these essays, it means more than simple remorse for bad deeds: it suggests a return to a life lived in relationship with God, a response to an awareness of God's presence.

The first essay, "The Power of Repentance," consists entirely of quotations from the Talmud and other Rabbinic texts. Several characteristics of the essay suggest that Heschel wove this collection together from memory, with no texts open before him. First, even though there are several quotations from the same sources, such as the Babylonian Talmud, Tractate Yoma 86a–b, they are out of order; Heschel seems to have retrieved them from memory according to his own internal logic. Second, there are a number of minor and a few major deviations from the versions of these quotations found in standard editions of the ancient texts. These deviations serve to highlight the overall precision of his quotations, making clear the remarkable depth and breadth of knowledge that Heschel was able to mine for his purposes. We have added citations to the original texts.

In the second essay, "The Meaning of Repentance," Heschel speaks not in the voice of the Talmud, but in his own passionate voice. It is an extremely personal exploration, a direct demand for relationship with God, for honest worship, and for walking the walk. In the end, it comes down to a plea for education: "It is up to the teachers among us to explain the meaning and content of repentance. Enlightenment about repentance is the central task of our time." The original German title of this essay, "*Die Marranen von Heute*," literally means "the Marranos of today." "Marrano" was a derogatory term used to refer to Jews of the Iberian Peninsula who were forced to convert to Christianity during the Inquisition but continued to practice Judaism secretly. Heschel accuses the German Jews in the 1930s of an opposite pretense: displaying a false front of Jewish identity while in their inner lives having no connection with God, no Jewish content or religious spark.

The final piece in this part, "Lights over the Sea," was published on November 29, 1937, corresponding to the twenty-fifth day of the Hebrew month of Kislev—the first day of Hanukkah. This story was Heschel's holiday gift to the Jews of Berlin. Instead of an exposition of the laws and customs of the season, Heschel offered something more in the spirit of the holiday: a tale to be told in the light of the menorah.

The Power of Repentance

(ROSH HASHANAH, 1936)

This essay was first published in the *Gemeindeblatt der jüdischen Gemeinde zu Berlin* on September 13, 1936.

Six things preceded the creation of the world, among them repentance. Since that hour it is said: You allow a person to repent to the point of contrition.[1]

A voice sounds from heaven: Repent, children of men![2]

Rabbi Eleazar said, "If someone has publicly offended a person and later wishes to reconcile, the offended person normally says, 'You have publicly shamed me and want to reconcile with me in private?! Go and get those people in front of whom you offended me, and then I will reconcile with you.' But this is not God's way: If a person stands in the marketplace and mocks and scorns Him, God will say to him, 'Repent in private, and I will accept you.'"[3]

Come and behold that the way of man is not God's way. If a person has been hurt with words, he may or may not be forgiving. But if someone has sinned, words will suffice for God to forgive. Further: He is grateful to him and takes the words of repentance as an offering.[4]

Prayer is like an immersion bath and repentance is like the sea. As an immersion bath opens and closes, so do the gates of prayer open and close. But the sea is always open, and so are the gates of repentance always open.[5]

Man is always frightened by his sins and returns remorsefully to the Holy One, blessed be He, asking forgiveness and reconciliation.

A live dog is better than a dead lion (Ecclesiastes 9:4). It is better to be a godless man who lives in the world and repents than a just man who has died in his sin.[6]

If a person has been completely righteous his entire life and falls away at the end, he has lost everything. "The righteousness of the righteous shall not save him when he transgresses."[7] If a person has been completely wicked his entire life and repents at the end, God accepts him: "nor shall the wickedness of the wicked cause him to stumble when he turns back from his wickedness."[8]

Rabbi Eliezer said, "Repent one day before your death." His students asked him, "Does a man know on which day he will die?" He answered, "All the more reason for him to repent today, since he may die tomorrow." In this way, he will have spent his entire life repenting.[9]

One who commits a sin and is ashamed of it will be forgiven all his sins.[10]

When is the sinner's repentance proved? When he once and then twice has the opportunity to commit a sin, and resists it.[11]

Rabbi Akiba taught: Sometimes it is said, "He decrees without punishment."[12] But then it is said, "He does not decree without punishment."[13] How do we reconcile these two sayings? For an offence against God, he waives the punishment, but for an offence against a person, he does not waive the punishment.[14]

Cain prayed to God: My guilt is too great for me to bear (Genesis 4:13). Because he repented, the punishment that he had been sentenced to was halved. Then his father, Adam, happened upon him. "What came of your situation?" he asked his son. "I have repented, and my punishment was halved." When Adam heard this, he hit himself on the head and said, "Such is the power of repentance, and I didn't know it! . . ."[15]

Great is the power of repentance, for it reaches as far as the throne of God.[16]

Great is the power of repentance, because it cancels a court's decree against the person.[17]

Great is repentance, because it lengthens the years of a person's life.[18]

Great is repentance, because it brings healing into the world.[19]

Great is repentance, because it leads to redemption.[20]

The Jews said to Isaiah, "Our teacher, Isaiah, how much of this night, of the banishment, has passed?" He responded, "Wait, I shall ask." When he had asked, he returned to them. They said, "What did the watchman say? What did the watchman of the world say?" Isaiah answered, "Morning comes and night comes also."[21] They said to him, "Night also? (Shall the present banishment be followed by others?)" He answered, "Not the way you think. Morning comes for the just and night for the godless." They said, "When (does morning come)?" He answered, "When you want it, He wants it." They said, "Then who is preventing it (redemption)?" He answered, "Repentance (i.e., lack of repentance)!"[22]

If the Jews do not repent, they will never be redeemed.[23]

God will place a king over them who will issue harsh edicts. Then they will repent and devote themselves to what is good.[24]

All the deadlines that have been calculated for the arrival of the Messiah have passed without it having happened. Now it depends on repentance and good works.[25]

Rabbi Meir said, "I had a son whom I loved very much, but he walked on evil paths, and I rejected him and turned him out of my house. But I set a deadline for him and said to him: If you repent, I will take you back into my house at any time. For the entire period that I set for him, he has been sitting and crying and screaming. We are God's children. Because of the arrogance that was within us, we angered Him and became obstreperous. He has rejected us, but also bound himself to us by an oath. If we repent, he will have mercy on us and let us return to our land. But if we walk on evil paths, he will not let us return to our land . . . ."[26]

It is said: Return, O Israel, to the Lord your God (Hosea 14:2). The power of repentance is great. If a person only resolves to repent, his essence ascends to God.[27]

If the Jews would repent for but *one* day, the Messiah would come immediately.[28]

Repentance is great, for when one person repents, God forgives the entire world.[29]

The Meaning of Repentance

(ROSH HASHANAH, 1936)

This essay was first published in the *Gemeindeblatt der jüdischen Gemeinde zu Berlin* on September 16, 1936.

The mystery of prayer on the days of Rosh Hashanah presents itself with a singular intimacy: it reveals itself to those who want to fulfill it, and eludes those who want only to know it.

Prayer on these days is a priestly service. When we pray, we fulfill a sacred function. At stake is the sovereignty and the judgment of God.

The world has fallen away from God. The decision of each individual person and of the many stands in opposition to God. Through our dullness and obstinacy, we, too, are antagonists. But still, sometimes we ache when we see God betrayed and abandoned.

Godliness is an absolute reality that exists through itself. It existed prior to the creation of the world and will survive the world in eternity. Sovereignty can exist only in a relationship. Without subordinates, this honor is abstract. God desired kingship, and from that will, creation emerged. But now the kingly dignity of God depends on us.

At issue is not an eschatological vision, a utopia at the end of time, or a kingdom in the beyond. Rather, we are talking about the present, the world that has been bequeathed to us, a kingdom of everyday life. We have to choose God as king; we have "to take the yoke of the kingdom of God upon ourselves."

Does this demand—the essence of Jewish law—signify an esoteric symbol, a mystical act? It signifies everyday action that is close at hand, this-worldly. The establishment or destruction of the kingly dignity of God occurs here and now, through and in us. In all that happens in the world, in thought, conversation, actions, the kingdom of God is at stake. Do we think of Him when we are anxious about ourselves or when, driven by apparent zeal for general concerns, we engage in life, whether deliberately or in a carefree way?

These days are dedicated to establishing God as king within us. The whole year long we call him "Holy God!"—on this day "Holy King!"

"God reigns over the nations; God is seated on His holy throne. The great of the peoples are gathered together. For the guardians of the earth belong to God" (Psalm 47:9–10, excerpts).

The deepest human longing is to be a thought in God's mind, to be the object of His attention. He may punish and discipline me, only let him not forget me, not abandon me. This single desire that links our life and our death will be fulfilled on the Days of Awe. The "Holy King" is a "King of Judgment." The season of Rosh Hashanah is the "Day of Memory," the "Day of Judgment."

Before the judgment and memory of God we stand. How can we prove ourselves? How can we persist? How can we be steadfast? Through repentance.

The most unassuming of all miracles is the miracle of repentance. It is not the same thing as rebirth; it is transformation, creation. In the dimension of time there is no going back. But the power of repentance causes time to be created backward and allows re-creation of the past to take place. Through the forgiving hand of

God, harm and damage that we have committed against the world and against ourselves will be extinguished, transformed into salvation.

God brings about this creation for the sake of humanity when a human being repents for the sake of God.

For many years we have experienced history as a judgment. What is the state of our repentance, of our "return to Judaism?"

Repentance is an absolute, spiritual decision made in truthfulness. Its motivations are remorse for the past and responsibility for the future. Only in this manner is it possible and valid.

Some people, in moments of enlightenment, believed they saw in the year 1933 an awakening to God and to the Jewish people, and hoped Jews would be heralds of repentance. Yet we have failed, those who stayed here just as much as those who emigrated. The enforced Jewishness still sits so loosely in many of us that a new wave of desertions could occur at any moment. The apostasy of the past is matched by the superficiality of today. Is this disappointment surprising? Repentance is a decision made in truthfulness, remorse, and responsibility. If, to be sure—as is often the case among us—instead of deliberate decision we have a coerced conversion; instead of a conscious truthfulness, a self-conscious conformity; instead of remorse over what has been lost, a longing for it; then this so-called return is but a retreat, a phase.

Return leading to ruin!—that is the apocalyptic *menetekel*[30] inscription on the walls of our houses.

Marranos of a new metamorphosis: Jewish on the outside, Marranos of different degrees multiply within our ranks. Such victims of insincerity—as historical experience teaches—can become tragic.

It is also deplorable when a spiritual movement deteriorates into bustling and pretense. It is unclean when a holy desire is misused by the selfishness of the efficient. When one wants to become a Jew because of the "situation," not out of honesty, the result is conflicted unhappiness. Jewishness cannot be feigned!

There is no return to Judaism without repentance before God. Faithfulness to Him and to the Jewish people to the point of ultimate sacrifice remains the fundamental idea of Jewish education.

We must recognize that repentance has yet to begin! Each of us must examine whether we are part of a movement forced on us by the environment or whether we are personally motivated, whether we are responding to pressure from outside or to an internal sense of urgency. At issue is not the sincerity of the motivation but the earnestness and honesty of its expression. This considered reflection has to become a permanent part of our consciousness.

Not everyone is capable of achieving self-examination. It is up to the teachers among us to explain the meaning and content of repentance. Enlightenment about repentance is the central task of our time.

It is a great good fortune that God thinks of us. We stand before the judgment and the memory of God. We know the reality of human judgment and we pray: Judge us, O God! We must stand firm before the judgment. The possibility to do so is given to us. Woe to us if it ceases; woe to us if God should forget us.

Lights over the Sea

(HANUKKAH, 1937)

This essay was first published in the *Gemeindeblatt der jüdischen Gemeinde zu Berlin* on November 29, 1937.

The sea was calm. The ship took its prescribed course. It was a smooth trip. On the deck the passengers lay somewhat lazily in their chaises longues and waited for the evening and the sound of the gong calling them to dinner. For several days they had watched the setting of the sun, but always with the same surprise at the unexpected. A fiery ball, a red, round disc stood in the sky. Suddenly it started to move and sank, clearly visible, into the ocean. It was as if unseen hands were pulling it down into the watery desert and no longer wished it to shine over the world. All that remained was a fading red sheen, a few clouds in the west reflected a delicate pink. And from the east darkness entered, almost abruptly, without transition; the twilight was short. Soon the first three stars began to sparkle.

"Now it's Hanukkah," said one of the three Jews.

They sat in their deck chairs just like the other passengers. They had been looking out to the sea, into the sun, endlessly into the sky. They had been thinking about this and that, about what had been and what would be. They were going far away in order to begin a new life. They were going to a country unknown to them. Earlier, in school, they would never have been able to remember the name of this country's capital.

"Now it's Hanukkah," he said again. The other two didn't answer. They looked silently into the emptiness. Now it was Hanukkah.

"Come!" said the oldest of the three into the silence. "Come! Let's light the candles!"

They got up from their chairs. It was difficult for them.

"Ach!" sighed the oldest one. A door slammed behind them. They looked at one another in alarm. It was only the wind that had moved it.

They were almost afraid of going to their cabins below deck. They walked over to the railing and looked down into the darkness of the water. Now and then it sprayed upward. From the portholes a light fell onto the sea. The stars were in the sky as ever. In full breaths the three sucked in the evening air. It was mild, almost humid. All three thought the same thing. The unspoken: no Hanukkah weather today. For that you need a cold wind whistling around the house and pressing against the creaking, leafless trees. For that you need a powdery snow that builds up in front of the house door. For that you need so much. Maybe also a carefree mood; maybe no fearful yearning for calm, nothing but the lights that look out onto the peace of the evening.

"Come," said the oldest once again. "Come, let's light the candles!"

They turned around and walked one behind the other, step by step. They stood against the wind. "Ach!" the oldest sighed. They felt that something had to stiffen in them, something had to stand straight for this hour. It's good not to think too much.

They went below deck and passed the gaunt American, who stepped aside, almost shyly. "Hello!" he called to them, this American, a "Hello" that contains so much. But they paid him no attention. Let him think: they speak to you all day long and now not a word. Funny people, these Jews. Indeed . . . .

They turned the light on in the cabin. They did it in an almost cautious way, as if they were going to unlock a secret. The three of them stood around the suitcase that contained the small gilded menorah. The oldest took it out; the two others followed his movements. It was precious, this menorah, a family piece, which no one would have ever imagined being lit at sea.

They didn't know where they should put the menorah. It was supposed to be placed, after all, at the window. That is the old Jewish custom: the world should see the candles; the world should see Hanukkah. There was no room and no support in front of the porthole. In front of the heavy, thick glass with its metal screws, a slanting sill sloped into the room.

"We'll take a suitcase, lay it flat, and put the menorah on it. Maybe it will hold," said the youngest of the three.

They took two small suitcases and succeeded in stacking them so that the menorah came directly in front of the porthole. The candles would be able to cast their light to the outside. But no one would see them. Even if a ship were to pass—unless it crossed very close to the course of the steamer, no one would notice the lights.

"It's a pity, actually," said the young man again. "We're stupid, actually. We take so much trouble to put the menorah in front of the window, and no one will see it."

"Ach, what do you know?" answered the oldest. "Would you have ever even lit your menorah before?"

The other was silent. But after a while he said, "That's a heavy accusation you're making. But it's not my fault that I never learned anything Jewish in my youth. It's my parents' fault. I would very much like to learn something today."

The older man gave no answer. All three looked at the menorah standing on the suitcase. Somehow the boat started to roll, and the menorah teetered a bit. "Ach," said the older man. Then there was, again, a heavy silence. Only the knocking of the machinery could be heard, uniform, dull, in an indifferent monotone.

"Light the candles!" commanded the older one. He himself took one of the golden-yellow wax candles out of the box that the younger man held out toward him. He gave it to the third man, who put it into the menorah as the *shammes*, with another candle on the left side of the first arm of the menorah.

They took out their caps. The older opened the prayer book and began to chant the ancient melody, the blessing over the lighting of the candles, as he had learned it from his father. Long forgotten days rose from the sea of forgetfulness. Large figures loomed, their familiar words sounding in their ears. But all of them were gone and far away: they weren't even in this world any longer, or if they were, one would probably never see them again. And the oldest recited that blessing of thanks that God has let us live until this time. He explained to the others just what that meant. The three of them stood around the menorah. In the cabin there was such a bright glow. Once long ago a light burned for eight days when it was supposed to last for only one. Eight days? In eight days we'll be at our destination, the three of them were thinking. At our destination? We're only at the beginning.

And then they sang Rock of Ages.

PART 5

Meditations

Context

The four short essays that close this collection were recently redis-covered. Susannah Heschel found the first two, "On Suffering" and "On the Seriousness of Prayer," among her father's personal papers. The typescripts are not dated, but presumably they were written before Heschel made his way to the United States, as he rarely wrote in German once he arrived in his new home. The third piece, "On Dreaming God's Dream," published in the Sep-tember 1941 edition of the *Bulletin* of Congregation Habonim in New York, is most likely Heschel's last text published in German. The final piece, "On Return," was discovered in the Duke University Archives. Though written in German, it was published in London in the December 1939 issue of the newsletter (*Mitteilungsblatt*) of the Theodor Herzl Society.

Each of these meditations is located squarely in the grief and loss experienced by Heschel and his fellow European Jews. But in each piece there is also evidence of profound optimism. In the face of mourning Heschel challenges himself and his readers to take spiritual action. He challenges us to experience suffering as a pathway to connection with community and connection with God: "Let us not be alone—in this realm of danger, in this time of calam-ity. Redemption begins in suffering." In writing about prayer, he focuses on authenticity—on resisting the escape of easy comfort, the distancing of irony, and the arrogance of self-satisfaction. His response to expulsion is a demand for return, not to the lands of the past, but to the ancient, sustaining, enduring spiritual reality of Jewish learning.

It is powerful to encounter his words about the redemptive possibilities of suffering, the challenge of authentic prayer, and the need for shared Jewish study at a time of such darkness and urgency.

On Suffering

Suffering confers neither a patent of nobility nor an obligation to purify oneself. It is a task that some may fail, but which may also be one's salvation. How is this task to be met? What can we create out of suffering?

To experience the intensity of one's own pain is not the meaning of suffering but rather a sign of danger. To be immersed in pain can lead one to the prison of the soul or to the freedom of community. It is left to the suffering person to recognize darkness or light.

Great and minor suffering, loss and unhappiness, deprivation and defeat—these lead us to the kingdom of true life, to community with others in harmony with God. In suffering, one experiences friendship, community, and God.

The path to community leads through personal suffering. Suffering is not the goal, but the path. It is narrow and steep, between the abyss and the peak. An ever-clearer view of humans and animals, of all creatures who are our brothers in suffering, is revealed to one who makes the ascent from pain and torment. All beings encounter one another on the paths of suffering, and we also encounter Him, who is with us in suffering. We have to be careful not to find a home in pain and to drown our thoughts in feelings. We should not enter into the maze of meditation on justice and injustice. The task given to the suffering person is to direct himself to suffering people, to see them in the fire of his own suffering, to see for others, both near and distant. Suffering breaks the circle of egotism in which our heart has been confined. The revelation of the Other is granted us. We see his life, we see his suffering.

That is the view into the distance. We see the direction of the straight path of suffering leading upward. Shedding the worship of the Self, giving up our illusions, we foster our ability to question our own conscience, to ask what is lasting in our own Self, what is essential in our own will, in our own life.

Slipping on this steep and narrow path of suffering is a constant danger. We will be misled by vanity, by a feeling of hatred. We misuse suffering to stir people up against the community, to spite the Spirit, to harden ourselves against meaning and direction. The Self becomes frozen in resentment. Instead of ascending the path, it allows itself to be seduced by a feeling of powerlessness and plummets into darkness. Instead of peace with the world, there arises discord with the universe.

Suffering is not a judgment but a test. Its outcome lies in our hands. God has determined to lead us into suffering, and man must choose which path to take within it.

What in our suffering matters? Judaism begins with the individual, and it is the individual who bears the full responsibility. Every person is Abraham's successor and the Messiah's herald. His endurance, his answer can signify a turning point. But we do not endure by what we give ourselves but rather by developing a sense for others who suffer and embarking on the path to the very root of our will. What lies at the deepest bottom of our will? Is it the craving for recognition? For power? For pleasure? Only the Self in abjection can responsibly inform us.

These cravings cannot constitute the foundations of our lives, spanning from the pangs of birth to death.

Suffering is the magic potion for remembering what is authentic in people, the spur to revolt against forgetting God, against the stupor of complacency. Pleasure, with its constant longing for stability and rest, can never hold our essence in its net. To build our lives on the alien, shaky teeter-totter of recognition would provide neither dignity nor equilibrium. Power, a theft from God's kingdom, is intoxication, not peace. One who forgets God can be forgotten by God. And when we are forgotten, life becomes a curse and the world a lair for murderers.

We do not live only in space and time but also in God's knowledge. Actions and objects do not only hold their human meaning and the weight of their measure. They also have their own value on the scales of holiness and their rank on the gauge of eternity.

He has sent us into suffering not in order to hurt us, but to bring us onto the path to Him, to Oneness. To live in the community of created beings is to re-form oneness with God on earth, to restore the unity of creation.

This is the witness that those who see—those who suffer—have to bear. The essence and the foundation are revealed in suffering, in the community of God and man: to live in His knowledge. And that is the prayer: Let us not be alone–in this realm of danger, in this time of calamity. Redemption begins in suffering.

We are tired of our broken lives, of our lives in individual cravings, fragmented and scattered. We are tired of our lives without center. An intact life begins when life in the world and life in God's knowledge are in harmony.

Space and time are not the world's limits. Life happens here and in God's knowledge.

If we truly look at ourselves and at others, in their seriousness, in their dignity, then we grasp a living, present thought of God's, then we think together with Him. Everything that occurs is also God's experience. To be self-conscious means to know oneself as a being known by God. When we understand beings in this way, we experience with God. When we misinterpret them, we falsify the divine message, the divine writ.

On the Seriousness of Prayer

Seriousness is a hallmark of prayer. There is no prayer without seriousness. But what does "seriousness" mean? This concept seems to include four aspects, namely: honesty, commitment, authenticity, and weightiness. When we speak seriously, we are honest; a serious word is committed; a serious word is authentic and weighty.

In prayer it is impossible to make false claims or pretenses, or to yield consciously to deception. Rather, everything depends on the measure of equality between intention and expression, on the harmony between conviction and awareness. Prayer without honesty is like scooping up water with a bottomless cup. A person praying means what he says.

Prayer is not an impulse, not something frivolous or private, but a highly committed and consequential action. To pray means to engage directly with God, to expose oneself to *Him*, to *His* will and *His* insight. The person who prays intends to change his life: he places his fate in the metaphysical dimension and more or less desists from arrogance. Without that intention, prayer remains a monologue and a private recitation. The recognition of divine rule, yes, *His* engagement as ruler of the world, and the affirmation of all obligations that entails—these form the daily exoteric mystery of Jewish prayer. Anthems and hymns of praise are not meditations but acts of engagement taken seriously.

Prayer is a weighty act. The word doesn't flow by but applies itself with its full weight from out of the deepest layer of personal life. It forms the Spirit; it determines the fate of the person who prays. Again and again, true prayer is an event in a person's life.

Prayer is not a game, not an illusion, not emulation, not the generation of one's own reflection, but an original act from which all elements spring, an occurrence that is real and true, in which nothing can be deceptive or manufactured. The use of slogans is the destruction of prayer.

Prayer is not an activity that is in itself restorative or pleasurable. It is demanding and strenuous. It does not spring, like play, from an excess of energy, but rather from suffering and humility. It is not an activity that, free and aimless, finds satisfaction in itself, but rather it is directed to a goal and should have consequences. There is no room for nonchalance. A person who prays is aware of his responsibility and concerned about the content of his prayer.

A person who prays wants to represent his concerns directly. An ironic stance toward their essential content is unthinkable. The expression of prayer flows forth, as if purely and directly from its intention, without the addition of any thoughts, whether central or ulterior.

There is a wariness, a diffidence about praying with words that are not canonized in the fixed prayer texts. Rarely do new prayers arise. For in prayer every word has weight and a mysterious validity, every word is a word of honor before God.

On Dreaming God's Dream

FOR ROSH HASHANAH 5702

And so, Eternal One, our God, we await You, that soon we may behold Your strength revealed in full glory sweeping away the abominations of the earth, obliterating idols, establishing in the world the sovereignty of the Almighty. All flesh will call out Your name—even the wicked will turn toward You. Then all who live on earth will recognize and understand that to You alone all knees must bend and allegiance be sworn. All will bow down and prostrate themselves before You, Eternal One, our God, honor Your glorious name, and accept the obligation of Your sovereignty. May You soon rule over them forever and ever for true dominion is Yours; You will rule in glory until the end of time. And it says: The Eternal One will reign over all the earth. On that day God shall be one, and his name shall be one.

This prayer, which is in the middle of the New Year holiday, is the true national anthem of the Jewish people. In it man is directed to what is coming. It is about the realization of God's kingdom, the goal of divine rule, and it is the prospect of this fulfillment that moves the praying person.

Everyone knows the condition of the soul that we call dreaming, or daydreaming. It is the yielding of feeling to something desired whose fulfillment is experienced imaginatively. That which has not yet happened but should happen is anticipated internally, in the dream. This is an important function of imagination in the order of life. In it the goals of the will are achieved. In it the future is creatively mapped out. It is in all seriousness the experiment of the soul, the experiment of inner history. It is a form of life in freedom.

In this sense life is dreaming, *dreaming for God*. For prayer is a mirroring in the human soul of divine intentions. Prayer begins with the awareness that the concerns of the person who prays are *His* concerns, or that they can be.

To mean *Him*—that is the central leitmotiv of all prayer. What does it mean to praise God if not to make His concerns our own? In the prayer, a praying person experiences his own concern as a concern of God's. Everything depends on what its content means for him. To pray is to feel a concern of God's or to have God feel a human concern.

Thus, one of the fundamental themes of prayer is: to accept *Him*, to make His goals our own concerns, to represent *His* challenge. The paradoxical act in blessing God means: to deliver reality up to Him. This is the fulfillment of an idea in the microcosm. And whoever prays for the realization of His kingdom has made Him king of his inner world. Prayer is its realization in the microcosm and at the same time more than prayer—it is a creative function of man unconfined by necessity, an act of *freedom*.

There are many stages in the effort to attain His will. First: to speak before Him in His way, then: to experience His agency, his aliveness in the world. That is how we succeed in understanding what exists and what is occurring from his perspective. We experience His interest in people and plead for help for His sake, gripped by that which is conveyed to us as His intention. The beginning is to think not only of ourselves but also of Him, simply to imagine His name. And the path leads through beauty and stillness from knowledge to knowledge, from understanding to understanding and to a common understanding with God.

At the beginning of every deed is the vision in which thoughts find their dreamlike fulfillment in which the future is fulfilled. And in prayer, too, we find the attainment of a hope, a hope that is shared by God and man. To pray is to dream in union with God, to see His visions.

On Return

Thousands of Jews are wandering the streets of foreign cities, chased from profession and home, with no path, no destination, no understanding of the meaning of their suffering, no comprehension of what has happened. These unhappy people, who are neither courageous enough for martyrdom nor strong enough to struggle and prevail, succumb to the fatal delusion that salvation comes from forgetting. In their despair, they fail to realize that as they flee they are losing the last remnants of their dignity and piling misery upon misery.

We have been challenged by the darkest powers, and no indignity could be more shameful than crawling away. What is our answer?

The answer to expulsion is return—to the Jewish community, to the Jewish spirit, to the Jewish land.

What has happened in all these years? After the World War we mourned the innumerable people who had lost their lives. But we didn't mourn the living who, in the turmoil of that time, had forfeited their conscience. In those years the voice of the heart was silenced, the vision of the spirit was frowned upon. To speak of goodness was deemed hypocrisy; the idea of love, ridiculous illusion. Reason was rendered impotent, and one didn't really know: Is evil evil? Is goodness good?

The beams came crashing down over a long time, but only few took note. The fissures were rent ever deeper, and, inside, walls fell. Those who lived within them died, and the neighbors thought it was no concern of theirs. Until everything collapsed. Now it concerns many nations.

Ghosts spread over the ruins of values. Power and hatred took up residence there, and soon they conquered an entire Reich. In this Reich there was no place for Jews. Why? Because independent of our will and our knowing, the meaning and duty of Jewish existence is to be a witness to the Spirit and to maintain the path of goodness.

So they were expelled. And the answer to expulsion is return. This means: to be a Jew. But what does being a Jew mean? Is it only a biblical fact, a matter of blood? Being a Jew is not a given of nature but a manifestation of the Spirit. Being a Jew is not only an inheritance but above all an act of acquisition. We inherit affinity and strength; we attain goal and achievement. We inherit the soul, but we attain the Spirit.

To be a Jew means to be of the Jewish Spirit, to be close to the Spirit that reveals itself in Jewish life and texts. Only in this closeness can Jewish action be realized, can Jewish achievement endure. And that is why the pursuit of Jewish texts and shared learning, and the path to one's own Jewish life, are a function of life, a question of Jews' being or not being.

NOTES

Introduction

1. Kaplan and Dresner, *Heschel*, 90.
2. Heschel, *Man's Quest for God*, 94–95.
3. Victor Klemperer, *Tagebücher, 1933–1942* (Berlin: Aufbau Verlag, 1995), 259.
4. Jay, "1920: The Free Jewish School," 396.
5. Eduard Strauss, "Das Lehrhaus," *Der Monat* 12, no. 9 (December 1936): 398.
6. "The Meaning of Repentance" was previously published in English translation in *Moral Grandeur and Spiritual Audacity*, edited by Susannah Heschel (Farrar, Straus and Groux).
7. Heschel, "The Spirit of Jewish Education," 62.

1. London

1. "Opening of the Term," Institute for Jewish Learning. AJHP, oversize box 5, folder 1.
2. *Mitteilungsblatt der Theodor Herzl Society*, no. 17 (February 2, 1940): 17.
3. *HaMizrachi* 2, no. 1 (November–December 1939): 28.
4. *The Jewish Chronicle*, 3, no. 696 (February 9, 1940): 23.
5. *Mitteilungsblatt der Theodor Herzl Society*, 3.
6. Heschel to Buber, February 7, 1940. Martin Buber Archive, National Library of Israel, MS var. 350.
7. Heschel to Buber, February 7, 1940.
8. Here Heschel has included the following phrases, presumably as placeholders for subsequent elaboration: "The penetration from outside. No resistance." Perhaps these phrases can be interpreted to mean that because Talmud scholars washed their hands of scientific study, new ideas had no chance to become integrated with Jewish thought. When they did enter the Jewish consciousness, their

impact was destructive, like the introduction of a germ into a sanitized environment with no inoculation.

9. In *The Earth Is the Lord's*, published in 1950, Heschel devotes a chapter to *pilpul*. There he reveals the revised view that may have been in his mind: "At times, the *pilpul* degenerated into hairsplitting dialectic and grappled with intellectual phantoms. Deviating from the conventional forms of logical soundness, it was bitterly attacked by some of the great rabbis. Yet, not only did the *pilpul* infuse new vitality into the study of Talmud, it stimulated ingenuity and independence of mind, encouraging students to create new out of old ideas. Over and above that, the storm of the soul that was held in check by rigorous discipline, the inner restlessness, found a vent in flights of the intellect. Thinking became full of vigor, charged with passion . . . . Ideas were like precious stones. The thought that animated them reflected a wealth of nuances and distinctions, as the ray of light passing through a prism produces the colors of the rainbow. Upon rotation, many-faceted ideas shed a glittering brilliance that varied in accordance with the direction in which they were placed against the light of reason. The alluring gracefulness, the variety of the polished ideas enlightened the intellect, dazzled the eye. Concepts acquired a dynamic quality, a color and a meaning that, at first thought, seemed to have no connection with one another. The joy of discovery, the process of inventing original devices, of attaining new inventions and new insights, quickened and elated the heart. This was not realistic thinking; but great art likewise is not a reproduction of nature, nor is mathematics an imitation of something that actually exists . . . . The world is sustained by unworldliness" (54).

10. The methodology of *pilpul* is based on strict logic and rationality, even though, when it comes to content, its practitioners are not particularly concerned with what Heschel called "truth and logical correctness" earlier in the paragraph.

11. Georg Simmel (1858–1918) was a German sociologist and philosopher.

12. Georg Simmel, *Schulpädagogik: Vorlesungen gehalten an der Universität Strassburg* (Osterwieck: Zickfeldt, 1922), 33.

13. *Talmud Bavli Hagigah* 15a.

14. *Talmud Yerushalmi Pe'ah* 2.4 [17a].

15. This is handwritten in Hebrew: עשו תעמולה בעד השכלה

16. The modern Hasidic movement originated in early eighteenth-century Ukraine with the expansion of the circle of disciples that gathered around Rabbi Israel ben Eliezer (1698–1760), a charismatic mystic also known as the Baal Shem Tov (Master of the Good Name). Though

it began among an elite group of pietists, the religiosity of the Baal Shem Tov and his circle was welcoming to uneducated, working class Jews: it did not require erudite text study for all adherents, it did not especially value asceticism, and it addressed the spiritual life of the individual in a new way. During the eighteenth and nineteenth centuries Hasidism spread throughout Eastern Europe. While the Hasidic aristocracy was extremely learned in the Jewish traditional mode, new educational strategies were needed to engage new, non-elite followers for the great rabbis, and these focused more on meeting their direct needs than on traditional learning for its own sake.

17. Heschel's review of the history of Jewish education begins with Maimonides (1138–1204). In Heschel's 1935 biography of Maimonides he describes the seminal medieval Jewish scholar as an educational reformer who "rejected the elaborate thinking that loses itself in the uncontrollable and endless effects of speculative intoxication; he rejected the tendency toward intricacy, complexity, and complication." Heschel describes the "rhythm of Jewish intellectual history" as alternating between systematic synthesis, as in the Mishnah, and expansive, open-ended analysis, as in talmudic *pilpul*. The synthesis of the Mishnah was followed by the expansiveness of the Talmud, until Maimonides swung the pendulum back to systematization with his *Mishneh Torah*, in which he collected, organized, and explicated the final decisions of talmudic law, without the arguments, sidebars, and multiple points of view that made the Talmud so hard to learn.

18. The next important synthesis after Maimonides's *Mishneh Torah* was Josef Karo's *Shulhan Aruch* (The set table), written in 1562 in the wake of the Jews' expulsion from Spain. Karo's goal was to make Jewish law accessible to the masses of Jews who were not elite scholars, presenting it as if laid out on a "set table," ready to be consumed. He went even further than Maimonides in the direction of practicality: he included only the laws relevant to contemporary Jewish life, leaving out issues of temple ritual and priestly conduct. Around 1800 Shneur Zalman of Liady, the founder of Habad Hasidism, wrote *Shulhan Aruch HaRav* (The set tale of the Rebbe) expanding Karo's text to include Hasidic commentaries and customs, also focusing on the law as lived, making it accessible and meaningful for the lay Jew.

19. *Aggadah* is nonlegal material in the Talmud and other Jewish texts— stories and lore. The *Zohar* is a mystical interpretation of the Bible, a foundational text of Kabbalah. The methods of studying *aggadah* or the *Zohar* are antithetical to *pilpul*.

20. A central element of Hasidism is a unique genre of storytelling, by and about Hasidic masters. The stories feature such things as mystical experiences, wonder-workers, and great feats of charity and kindness.

21. Contemporary scholar of Jewish mysticism Arthur Green explains this phrase as it applied to the Hasidic masters: "In reading the Torah as well as the works of previous mystical masters, they sought to approach everything *al derech ha-avodah*, 'in the way of service.' Theirs is a practical rather than a theoretical mysticism. 'How can this concept, verse, or teaching help me understand myself, so that I can better serve God?' was their constant question." Arthur Green, *Ehyeh: A Kabbalah for Tomorrow* (Woodstock VT: Jewish Lights, 2004), 92.

22. The insularity of Hasidic culture impeded the reception of the great innovations of Western thinking. Heschel particularly mentions "forms" and "language"—two lenses that the *Wissenschaft* movement used to explore ancient texts in a radically new way.

23. Despite the promise that some Jews saw in the European Enlightenment, the dawn of the nineteenth century did not usher in an era in which Judaism was generally respected and Jews were accepted as full participants in European society. A circle of young Jews who had made their way through German universities, most notably Leopold Zunz (1794–1886) at the University of Berlin, perceived that in the post-Enlightenment world academic study had the power to strengthen meaning and value. They proposed that the stature of Judaism in the eyes of both Jews and non-Jews could be transformed by the development of a new academic discipline that would apply the methods of objective scientific study to the Jewish past. They gave the name *Wissenschaft des Judentums* (the Science of Judaism) to their program of research and education that undertook to examine Judaism through the objective lens of historical criticism.

24. Max Wiener (1882–1950) was a German Jewish rabbi and philosopher.

25. Abraham Geiger and other *Wissenschaft* thinkers, believed that the Talmud originally represented a fluid process, responsive to historical change; its canonization as fixed and finished imposed rigidity on the law and prevented the free interchange with other cultural and intellectual streams.

26. Abraham Geiger (1810–74) was a founding father of Reform Judaism.

27. Eduard Meyer, *Humanistische und geschichtliche Bildung* (Berlin: Weidmannsche Buchhandlung, 1907), 35.

28. Konrad Burdach, *Reformation, Renaissance, Humanismus* (Berlin: Gebrüder Paetel, 1918), 98.

29. The Hebrew word *haskalah* refers to the Jewish response to the European Enlightenment, beginning in the second half of the eighteenth century. In the vanguard of that response was the German Jewish philosopher Moses Mendelssohn (1729–86), who urged Jews to take advantage of every opportunity to leave the confines of their traditional communities and make their way into the world of secular European culture. The impact of the Enlightenment in Eastern Europe was delayed by several decades, and by the time the Haskalah took hold in Poland, Russia, and Lithuania, in the mid-nineteenth century, it had acquired a somewhat different character. Compared to their German counterparts, Jews in the East were less eager to become part of the non-Jewish intellectual culture; they concentrated instead on bringing Enlightenment values into Jewish discourse. *Maskilim* (adherents of Haskalah) in such urban centers as Vilna undertook educational reforms that added science, mathematics, and languages to the curricula of Jewish schools. The study of Hebrew was treasured, both as the language of the Bible and as a new modern idiom. Though the German Haskalah had rejected Yiddish, here it became the conduit for bringing modern sensibilities to the Jewish masses. New genres of Yiddish and modern Hebrew literature thrived.

30. In the manuscript, Heschel has handwritten the Hebrew phrase בת השמים—"daughter of heaven"—and the German (from the Greek) word "Pathos." The former was a phrase used to express the optimism felt by Eastern European Jews at the dawning of the Jewish Enlightenment. The latter is a crucial concept in Heschel's understanding of the relationship between God and humans. In his work on the prophets, he used "pathos" to characterize the ability of the prophetic consciousness to empathize with the Divine. The concept of "divine pathos," God's ardent concern for humanity, became a cornerstone of Heschel's mature theology.

31. Heschel's personal *haskalah* (enlightenment)—his secondary school experience at the Real-Gymnasium in Vilna—included a strong emphasis on the study of languages and linguistics.

32. Aloys Fischer, "Pädagogische Soziologie," in *Aloys Fischer Leben und Werk* (München: Bayerischer Schulbuch-Verlag, 1950), 1:137

33. The classicist Werner Jaeger describes *kalos kagathos* in Greek thought as "the physical and spiritual education of the whole personality . . . patterned on an ideal which combined the highest qualities of body and soul." The goal of this education is to develop "the chivalrous ideal of the complete human personality, harmonious in mind and body,

foursquare in battle and speech, song and action." Werner Jaeger, *Paideia: The Ideals of Greek Culture,* trans. Gilbert Highet (Oxford: Basil Blackwell, 1946), 1:287, 1:62.

34. Wilhelm von Humboldt (1767–1835) founded the University of Berlin (now Humboldt University of Berlin) in 1810.

35. In the Bible, Moloch was the god to whom the surrounding nations would sacrifice their children, a practice that the Israelites were forbidden to emulate. Heschel implies that the education of the day amounted to the sacrifice of children for the sake of the Volk—literally, the people, here perhaps, communal productivity.

36. Eduard Spranger (1882–1963) was a German philosopher and psychologist.

37. Ernst Krieck, *Nationalpolitische Erziehung* (Leipzig: Armanen-Verlag, 1933), 2.

38. Oswald Spengler, *Jahre der Entscheidung* (München: Beck, 1933), 163.

2. Personalities in Jewish History

1. *Talmud Yerushalmi Ta'anit* 4.2 [68a] and *Genesis Rabbah* 98.8.

2. In Rabbinic literature, the *nasi* is usually referred to using a special honorific, "Rabban"— "our master," rather than the more common "Rabbi"—"my master." Heschel uses "Rabbi" rather than "Rabban," and our translation follows suit.

3. Present-day Hebrew editions are usually published as multivolume sets. Herbert Danby's 1933 English translation fits in one volume of eight hundred very densely filled pages.

4. Josephus and Graetz describe a similar incident in a different place and time. According to them, it was not in Jerusalem but in Gamla—a city in the Golan overlooking the Sea of Galilee—that soldiers stormed the low roofs of houses, causing them to collapse and resulting in many Roman casualties. The Romans laid siege to Gamla in 67 CE, a few years before the siege of Jerusalem. See *Wars of the Jews,* 4.1.4, in Josephus, *Complete Works,* 523; and Graetz, *History of the Jews,* 2:289.

5. *Talmud Bavli Gittin* 56a–b includes a description of these events.

6. This quotation is from *Wars of the Jews,* 5.11.1, in Josephus, 565.

7. In this context, "Mishnah" refers to the orally transmitted traditions that would eventually be redacted by Rabbi Judah Hanasi, and "Talmud" refers to the discussions of these traditions among the Rabbis.

8. *Talmud Bavli Sukkah* 28a and *Talmud Bavli Bava Batra* 134a. Where Heschel has "scholars," the Talmud has "scribes." Where Heschel has "astronomy" and "geometry," the Talmud has "calendrics"—the

calculation of dates according to the overlapping solar and lunar calendars—and *gematria*—the numerological interpretation of Hebrew words and letters. Heschel also leaves out from his list two tools of Rabbinic legal interpretation that are included in the Talmud's versions: *kal vahomer*—*a fortiori* argument, that is, argument from a lesser case to a more weighty case—and *gezerah shava*—the linking together of otherwise unrelated biblical passages based on the use of similar words or phrases.

9. *Talmud Bavli Gittin* 56a; *Avot de Rabbi Natan A*, chap. 4.

10. *Talmud Bavli Gittin* 56a–b; *Avot de Rabbi Natan A*, chap. 4. In *Avot de Rabbi Natan*, Vespasian grants Rabbi Johanan permission to build a community of study and practice in Yavne because he has heard reports that Rabbi Johanan urged the Jews to surrender to the Romans rather than let Jerusalem be destroyed. In the *Talmud Bavli Gittin* version, permission is granted because Rabbi Johanan correctly predicts Vespasian's imminent appointment as emperor.

11. According to the Talmud (Bavli Yoma 39b; Yerushalmi Yoma 6.3 [43c]), in the years before its destruction, the Temple predicted its own demise. Here, Rabbi Johanan scolds the Temple for frightening the people. He dismisses its prediction as old, well-known news announced long ago by the prophet Zechariah. The passage refers to two background concepts. First, Leviticus 16 describes a ritual in which a goat is sent into the wilderness to expiate the community's sins. The Talmud (Bavli Yoma 67a) explains that in temple times this ritual involved dividing a crimson thread in two, then tying half to the horns of the goat and half to the doorway of the Temple. If the ritual was efficacious and the sins were wiped away, then the red string at the Temple would turn white. If the goat did not reach the wilderness, or if the atonement was not accepted, the string remained red. Second, the Talmud (Bavli Shabbat 22b) reports that the westernmost branch of the seven-branched menorah in the Temple had a special quality. Though it held the same amount of oil as the other branches, it burned longer, allowing all the other lights to be lit from it when they were refilled. The passage quoted here explains that during the administration of a righteous leader, the red string always turned white and the westernmost lamp always stayed lit, while in ordinary times these auspicious signs were only sometimes revealed.

12. *Avot de Rabbi Natan B*, chap. 31. The saying is also quoted in *Talmud Bavli Megillah* 31b and *Talmud Bavli Nedarim* 40a, but in the latter it is attributed to Rabbi Shimon ben Eleazar.

13. See, e.g., Jeremiah 23:13–14.

14. This prohibition is found in *Mishnah Ḥagigah* 2.1 without attribution. In three other sources—the parallel Tosefta passage, *Talmud Bavli Ḥagigah* 14b, and *Talmud Yerushalmi Ḥagigah* 2.1 [77a]—Rabbi Johanan quotes this rule in rebuffing a student who wishes to engage in the mystical study of God. However, Rabbi Johanan's resistance to mysticism is limited: in all three sources, when his students go on to expound on mystical matters themselves, Rabbi Johanan praises them passionately.

15. *Talmud Bavli Sukkah* 28a.

16. *Minor Tractates Sofrim* 16:88. According to the story in Sofrim, it was actually a fly, not a gull.

17. *Minor Tractates Sofrim* 16:88.

18. *Talmud Bavli Sukkah* 28a.

19. *Talmud Bavli Berachot* 17a.

20. In the sources (*Tosefta Bava Kama* 7.5; *Talmud Yerushalmi Kiddushin* 1.2 [59d]), this is presented as criticism of the slave who would choose to remain with his master even after the seventh year, when by biblical law he has the right to go free (Exodus 21:2–6).

21. *Tosefta Bava Kama* 7.6; *Mechilta deRabbi Ishmael*, Yitro, BaHodesh 11.

22. *Mechilta deRabbi Ishmael*, Yitro, BaHodesh 11.

23. *Sifre Deuteronomy, piska* 192.

24. *Talmud Bavli Sukkah* 28a.

25. *Avot de Rabbi Natan B*, chap. 28; *Talmud Yerushalmi Nedarim* 5.6 [39b].

26. *Mishnah Avot* 2.8.

27. *Talmud Bavli Berachot* 28b.

28. *Mishnah Sotah* 9.15.

29. This statement appears a number of times in Rabbinic literature: *Tosefta Hagigah* 2.9, *Tosefta Sotah* 14.9, *Talmud Yerushalmi Hagigah* 2.2 [78a], *Talmud Bavli Sotah* 47b, *Talmud Bavli Sanhedrin* 88b. "Ever since the disciples of Shammai and Hillel became many who had not served [their teachers] adequately, disputes became many in Israel and the Torah became like two Torahs."

30. Heschel must be referring to the Sadducees, who lived in the generations preceding Rabbi Gamliel, and not to the Karaites, who were active in the medieval era. The Sadducees were a group of Second Temple priests who rejected the validity of the Oral Law, claiming that only the Bible and not Rabbinic decree had legitimate authority. Based on biblical law, they understood the temple ritual—and their own priestly function—as the central features of Jewish practice. After the fall of

the Temple, the Sadducees ceased to exist as a group. The Karaites, a medieval sect, also rejected the Oral Law, including the Talmud. Many speculate that this sect may have emerged from the Sadducees.

31. *Tosefta Berachot* 6.18, which uses the Hebrew term *bor*, not *am ha'aretz*, to refer to an uneducated person.

32. *Talmud Yerushalmi Shabbat* 16.3 [15d].

33. *Talmud Bavli Shabbat* 138b. The biblical quotation is from Amos 8:11.

34. Heschel uses the term "particularism" here to refer to the one-sided, uncompromising positions that Rabbi Gamliel sought to reconcile.

35. *Talmud Bavli Berachot* 28a.

36. *Mishnah Berachot* 4.3 quotes Rabbi Gamliel as the source of the obligation to recite daily the set of prayers known as the Eighteen Benedictions.

37. *Talmud Bavli Berachot* 28b. Noting that the prayer called "Eighteen Benedictions" actually consists of nineteen sections, the Talmud explains that after the order of the prayers was established Rabbi Gamliel noticed that there was no prayer against heretics, so an additional benediction was composed and inserted.

38. See, e.g., *Mishnah Rosh Hashanah* 2.8, which describes charts of the phases of the moon hanging on Rabbi Gamliel's walls.

39. Traveling, carrying burdens, and using money are forbidden on the Day of Atonement.

40. The story is told in *Mishnah Rosh Hashanah* 2.9. Rabbi Joshua concedes because he becomes convinced that the law as decided by the court (in this case, the opinion of Rabbi Gamliel) becomes the true law and cannot be later overturned. The final line, "Praise be to the age in which the great obey the small," is added in the Gemara in *Talmud Bavli Rosh Hashanah* 25b.

41. *Talmud Bavli Eruvin* 13b; *Talmud Yerushalmi Berachot* 1.2 [3b].

42. Among the stories of excommunication is the narrative in *Talmud Bavli Bava Metzia* 59b. There Rabbi Gamliel excommunicates his brother-in-law, Rabbi Eliezer, and annuls all his previous rulings. In the end, Rabbi Gamliel's death is attributed to the power of Rabbi Eliezer's agonized prayers for mercy.

43. The "speaker for the patriarch" was his translator (Hebrew: *turgemon*). The patriarch spoke in a quiet voice, and in order for him to be heard in the large chamber his words were broadcast, and sometimes expanded on, by an assistant—a speaker with a booming voice. Demanding that the speaker desist was like unplugging the patriarch's microphone.

44. *Talmud Bavli Berachot* 27b. The story continues for the next several paragraphs.
45. Rabbi Eleazar ben Azaria's wife is concerned that he will be disrespected because he is young. The white hairs produced by this miracle will make him seem more mature.
46. *Talmud Bavli Berachot* 27b–28a. Heschel skips a section in which Rabbi Gamliel dreams that the students he excluded were in fact unworthy. The Talmud then comments that they really were worthy and that the dream was sent just to make him feel better.
47. *Talmud Bavli Berachot* 28a, continued.
48. *Talmud Bavli Berachot* 28a, conclusion.
49. *Talmud Bavli Sanhedrin* 104b.
50. *Talmud Bavli Shabbat* 151b.
51. *Mishnah Berachot* 2.7. "When Tabi his slave died, he accepted condolences for him. His disciples said to him, 'Did you not teach us, our Rabbi, that one does not accept condolences for slaves?' He said to them, 'My slave Tabi was not like other slaves: He was worthy.'"
52. *Talmud Bavli Bava Metzia* 59b.
53. *Talmud Bavli Sotah* 49b. Mirrors were considered a sign of vanity unseemly for a man.
54. An illustration of Rabbi Gamliel's willingness to "serve" is found in *Talmud Bavli Kiddushin* 32b, where he serves drinks to those below him in rank.
55. The sources contain several variations on this story: *Tosefta Shabbat* 7.18, *Minor Tractates Semahot* 8.6, *Talmud Bavli Avodah Zarah* 11a. In each of them the royal treatment consists of the non-Jewish practice of burning objects at the burial of a king, performed by a proselyte whom Rabbi Gamliel has converted.
56. *Talmud Bavli Mo'ed Katan* 27b; *Talmud Bavli Ketubot* 8b.
57. *Talmud Bavli Menahot* 29b, translated somewhat freely by Heschel.
58. *Pesikta Rabbati, piska* 14, portion Parah. The original text reads: "Things that were not revealed to Moses were revealed to Rabbi Akiba."
59. The Mishnah of Rabbi Akiba is mentioned a few times in Rabbinic literature, including in *Mishnah Sanhedrin* 3.4. Since there is no evidence that a text by this name existed, the phrase may refer to Akiba's role in shaping and organizing the material that eventually became the Mishnah.
60. *Sifre Deuteronomy, piska* 48.
61. Lydda (also known as Lod) was a town in southern Palestine. A number

of talmudic conversations are reported to have taken place in the upper story of Nitsa's house there.

62. A variant on *Talmud Bavli Kiddushin* 40b. The original text ends somewhat differently: "Rabbi Tarfon and the elders were once reclining in the upper story of Nitsa's house in Lydda. This question was raised before them: Is study greater, or is action greater? Rabbi Tarfon responded and said, 'Action is greater.' Rabbi Akiba responded and said, 'Study is greater.' Then all of them responded and said, 'Study is greater, for it leads to action.'"

63. *Pilpul*, the Hebrew word for "pepper," refers to a style of talmudic argumentation that involves sharp analysis of words and dissection of details. Sometimes criticized as casuistic and hairsplitting, sometimes lauded for its logic and rigor, *pilpul* is still a staple in many contemporary institutions of traditional Jewish learning.

64. The word *talmud* literally means "teaching." In this passage, Heschel uses that term to refer to the developing body of Oral Law that in approximately 500 CE would mature to become the text known as the Talmud, comprising the Mishnah supplemented by later discussions and commentaries.

65. *Talmud Bavli Berachot* 61b. Heschel concludes this story at the end of the essay.

66. *Talmud Bavli Ketubot* 62b–63a. Heschel's translation is somewhat free. Akiba's comment means that it is only because of his wife's urging that Akiba and his disciples had the opportunity to study, and thus to reach their present state of wisdom.

67. *Talmud Bavli Yevamot* 16a.

68. *Talmud Bavli Kiddushin* 66b.

69. *Talmud Bavli Mo'ed Katan* 21b.

70. This is described in *Talmud Bavli Kiddushin* 27a.

71. A variant on *Talmud Bavli Pesahim* 112a. Other interpreters, including Marcus Jastrow, understand the phrase to mean, "Make your sabbath like a weekday rather than become dependent upon another person [for elegant food]."

72. *Genesis Rabbah* 24.7; *Talmud Yerushalmi Nedarim* 9.4 [41c].

73. *Mishnah Makkot* 1.11.

74. The passage is from the midrash collection *Lamentations Rabbah* 2.4, which quotes Numbers 24:17—"A star will arise from Jacob, a scepter shall come up from Israel, smashing the brow of Moab." Rabbinic texts often decode "Moab" as a reference to Rome.

75. The verse reads: "You shall love the Lord your God with all your heart

and with all your soul . . . ." Rabbi Akiba interprets the second clause to mean that you must love God even as God is taking your soul. The word translated "soul" is *nefesh*, which can also mean "life."

76. *Talmud Bavli Berachot* 61b—slightly abridged by Heschel.

77. *Sifre Deuteronomy, piska* 80.

78. *Talmud Bavli Berachot* 63a.

79. *Talmud Bavli Rosh Hashanah* 19a.

80. *Talmud Bavli Rosh Hashanah* 19a.

81. *Talmud Bavli Sotah* 49b; *Talmud Bavli Bava Kama* 83a.

82. Some examples: *Talmud Bavli Berachot* 25a and 40a (medicine); *Talmud Bavli Shabbat* 128b (zoology).

83. *Talmud Bavli Berachot* 63a–b. A continuation of the story.

84. *Talmud Bavli Kiddushin* 40b.

85. *Mishnah Avot* 1.17.

86. *Talmud Bavli Sanhedrin* 14a specifically mentions that Rabbi Shimon did not base interpretations on the accusative case marker, *et*, while Rabbi Akiba was famous for placing interpretive weight on this and other seemingly irrelevant particles of Hebrew grammar. See, e.g., *Talmud Bavli Kiddushin* 57a and *Talmud Bavli Hagigah* 12a. In *Talmud Bavli Menahot* 29b, Akiba is described as one who derives "heaps and heaps of laws" from the calligraphic flourishes that scribes traditionally add to the letters in the Torah scroll.

87. *Sifre Deuteronomy, piska* 25.

88. This is the continuation of the conversation about the relative value of learning and doing in *Talmud Bavli Kiddushin* 40b.

89. Rabbi Shimon ben Yochai was a student of Rabbi Akiba.

90. *Talmud Bavli Berachot* 35b.

91. *Talmud Bavli Shabbat* 33b, paraphrased.

92. This idea is alluded to in *Talmud Bavli Bava Batra* 60b.

93. See part 2 note 61 herein.

94. *Talmud Bavli Sanhedrin* 74a; *Talmud Yerushalmi Sanhedrin* 3.5 [21b].

95. *Talmud Bavli Berachot* 61b.

96. *Talmud Bavli Shabbat* 151b.

97. *Sifre Deuteronomy, piska* 76.

98. See, e.g., *Talmud Bavli Gittin* 12a.

99. The Valley of Ginosar is located on the northwest shore of the Sea of Galilee.

100. The full passage is as follows: "If, along the road, you chance upon a bird's nest, in any tree or on the ground, with fledglings or eggs and the mother sitting over the fledglings or the eggs, do not take the mother

together with her young. Let the mother go, and take only the young, in order that you may fare well and have a lengthened life."

101. *Talmud Yerushalmi Hagigah* 2.1 [77b].

102. *Talmud Yerushalmi Hagigah* 2.1 [77b]. According to Rabbinic lore, Judah the Baker was tortured to death during the Hadrianic persecutions as punishment for defying the prohibition against teaching Torah.

103. The angel Metatron appears in ancient apocryphal texts and medieval Jewish mystical works as a kind of go-between to whom God relinquished some level of control of the created world. In the "Narrative of the Ten Martyrs" (*Midrash Eleh Ezkerah,* translated in David Stern, *Rabbinic Fantasies, Philadelphia: Jewish Publication Society, 1990*), the self-sacrifices of the martyrs in this world are paralleled by sacrifices of their righteous souls by Metatron in the heavenly realm, effecting atonement for the sins of Israel in the post-temple era. This may be the "later tale" to which Heschel refers. The image of Metatron sacrificing the souls of the righteous also appears in *Numbers Rabbah* 12.12.

104. *Talmud Bavli Hagigah* 15a.

105. *Talmud Bavli Hagigah* 15a. A single word means both "turn back" and "repent" in Hebrew (*shuvu*) and in German (*Umkehr*). Since there is no comparable word in English, we are unable to reproduce the pun in this translation.

106. *Talmud Bavli Hagigah* 15a.

107. *Mishnah Avot* 4.2

108. The idea that suffering is a "chastisement of love" is discussed in *Talmud Bavli Berachot* 5a.

109. *Mishnah Avot* 4.20.

110. According to Rabbinic tradition, Rabbi Akiba did not start learning until age forty (*Genesis Rabbah* 100.10; *Avot de Rabbi Natan A,* chap. 6; *Avot de Rabbi Natan B,* chap. 12).

111. *Talmud Bavli Sanhedrin* 90a quotes Rabbi Akiba as saying that one who reads noncanonical books "has no share in the world to come."

112. *Talmud Bavli Hagigah* 15a.

113. *Talmud Bavli Hagigah* 15a.

114. *Mishnah Kiddushin* 4.14. It is quoted there in the name of Rabbi Nehorai, not Rabbi Meir, but elsewhere (*Talmud Bavli Eruvin* 13b) the Talmud declares that these are two names for one person.

115. *Talmud Yerushalmi Hagigah* 2.1 [77b].

116. *Talmud Bavli Hagigah* 15a.

117. Rabbi Meir's reading of the verse uses a play on words. The Hebrew

of the verse is difficult, but in context it probably means "You return man to dust," as in the NJPS translation.

118. *Talmud Yerushalmi Hagigah* 2.1 [77b].

119. *Mishnah Avot* 6.1, quoting Rabbi Meir.

120. *Talmud Bavli Eruvin* 13b. The talmudic passage offers this explanation of why he is called "Meir" even though that is not his real name. The passage also offers various opinions about his real name: Rabbi Nehorai, Rabbi Nehemia, or Rabbi Eleazar ben Arak.

121. *Talmud Bavli Sanhedrin* 86a: "The *stam* [anonymous voice] of the Mishnah is Rabbi Meir; the *stam* of the Tosefta is Rabbi Nehemiah; the *stam* of the Sifra is Rabbi Judah; the *stam* of the Sifre is Rabbi Shimon; and all of them are according to the view of Rabbi Akiba." This is taken to mean that each of these students of Rabbi Akiba compiled a preliminary collection that was eventually redacted into the specified book. Thus, Rabbi Meir is the original collector of the material in the Mishnah.

122. The discussion of Rabbi Meir beginning his learning in one House of Learning, then switching to the other, then back to the first is found in *Talmud Bavli Sotah* 20a and *Talmud Bavli Eruvin* 13a.

123. *Talmud Bavli Sotah* 20a and *Talmud Bavli Eruvin* 13a.

124. *Talmud Bavli Gittin* 67a.

125. *Ecclesiastes Rabbah* 2.17.

126. *Midrash Mishlei* (Proverbs) 31.10. *Yalkut Shimoni* (Proverbs 964). Commentary on *eishet hayil,* "a woman of valor."

127. *Talmud Bavli Sanhedrin* 38b–39a: "When Rabbi Meir would discuss the portion, a third was *halachah,* a third was *aggadah,* and a third was parables. And Rabbi Johanan said that Rabbi Meir had three hundred fox parables, and we have only three left, commenting on these verses: Ezekiel 18:2—'Parents eat sour grapes and their children's teeth are blunted'; Leviticus 19:36—'[You shall have] an honest balance, honest weights'; Proverbs 11:8—'The righteous man is rescued from trouble, and the wicked man takes his place.'" The Talmud does not record the content of these fables, but Rashi, writing many centuries later, includes in his talmudic commentary a story about a clever fox who saves the Jews from a vicious but foolish wolf.

128. In one talmudic tale (*Talmud Bavli Avodah Zarah* 18a), Rabbi Meir takes the form of a Roman knight to save his wife's sister from forced prostitution.

129. *Aher,* meaning "other," is Elisha ben Abuyah's nickname.

130. *Talmud Yerushalmi Hagigah* 2.1 [77a], *Ruth Rabbah* 6.4, and *Ecclesiastes Rabbah* 7.8.

131. The three leadership roles in the Sanhedrin were *nasi* (variously translated as "patriarch," "prince," or "president"), *hacham* (chief sage), and *av beit din* (head of the legal court). These three positions originally held equal prestige, until Rabbi Shimon ben Gamliel introduced a hierarchy that placed the *nasi* above the others.

132. Uktzin, the last of the Mishnah's sixty-three tractates, discusses ritual impurities related to the stems and peels of fruits and vegetables. Its obscurity is underscored by the fact that it is not treated in the Gemara by either the Talmud Bavli or the Talmud Yerushalmi.

133. *Talmud Bavli Horayot* 13a–b.

134. *Talmud Bavli Sanhedrin* 24a.

135. *Talmud Bavli Kiddushin* 52b.

136. *Talmud Bavli Eruvin* 13b.

137. Some scholars understand "Asia" here to refer to the area at the southern tip of the modern State of Israel that is now Eilat. Others take it to mean Asia Minor, which roughly corresponds to present-day Turkey.

138. *Talmud Bavli Horayot* 13b.

139. *Talmud Bavli Horayot* 14a. According to this passage, instead of the expression "Rabbi Meir said," Rabbi Judah Hanasi would say, "It was taught in the name of Rabbi Meir."

140. In *Talmud Bavli Berachot* 17a, this synopsis of Job is attributed to Rabbi Johanan, not Rabbi Meir. In the later midrash collection *Yalkut Shimoni* (Job 928), Rabbi Johanan offers it as a quote from Rabbi Meir.

141. *Genesis Rabbah* 9.5. This midrash examines the phrase *v'hinei tov m'od* in Genesis 1:31: "God saw all that he had made. And behold: Very good!" Playing with sounds, Rabbi Meir substitutes *mot* (dying) for *m'od* (very), yielding "And behold: Dying is good."

142. *Talmud Bavli Sanhedrin* 98b.

143. *Talmud Bavli Ketubot* 104a.

144. *Talmud Bavli Avodah Zarah* 10a–b records a series of tales about a close relationship between Rabbi Judah Hanasi and the Roman emperor known as Antoninus.

145. *Talmud Bavli Shabbat* 113b.

146. Some tales in which Rabbi weeps are found in *Talmud Bavli Hagigah* 15b, *Talmud Bavli Hullin* 7b, and *Talmud Bavli Avodah Zarah* 10b, 17a, and 18a.

147. *Talmud Yerushalmi Ta'anit* 4.2 [68a] and *Genesis Rabbah* 98.8 cite the tradition that Hillel, an ancestor of Rabbi Judah Hanasi, was descended from King David, though this claim is more folkloric than historical.

148. *Talmud Bavli Ketubot* 103b. This is Rabbi's advice to his son from his deathbed.

149. *Talmud Bavli Sanhedrin* 5b.
150. *Talmud Yerushalmi Sanhedrin* 1.2 [19a].
151. *Talmud Bavli Makkot* 10a.
152. *Talmud Bavli Bava Batra* 8a.
153. In this context, "Mishnah" refers to the orally transmitted traditions that would eventually be redacted by Rabbi Judah Hanasi, and "Talmud" refers to the discussions of these traditions that took place among the Rabbis.
154. *Talmud Bavli Bava Batra* 8a.
155. *Talmud Bavli Sotah* 49a (*Mishnah Sotah* 9.15).
156. *Talmud Bavli Bava Metzia* 84b.
157. *Talmud Bavli Sanhedrin* 5b.
158. *Talmud Bavli Gittin* 59b.
159. *Mishnah Avot* 6.8.
160. *Talmud Bavli Berachot* 57b.
161. *Talmud Bavli Sukkah* 26b.
162. *Talmud Bavli Nedarim* 50b.
163. *Talmud Bavli Bava Metzia* 85a (paraphrased). A similar story is found in *Genesis Rabbah* 33.3.
164. *Talmud Yerushalmi Rosh Hashanah* 2.1 [58a]. The start of each new month was determined based on the testimony of valid witnesses who had seen the sliver of the new moon. The news was then disseminated by lighting beacon fires on successive mountaintops. According to the talmudic passage, Rabbi Judah Hanasi made the validity test for witnesses far less stringent, and eliminated the beacon fire system.
165. In Exodus 23, Leviticus 25, and Deuteronomy 15, the Bible specifies that every seventh year is to be a year of "release": a sabbatical year in which fields lie fallow and debts are cancelled. Leviticus 25 prescribes an additional release after seven cycles of seven years: the fiftieth year is a "jubilee" in which slaves are set free and land that has been sold reverts to the ownership of the family to whom it had been assigned when the Israelites arrived in the Promised Land. Rabbi Judah sought to ease the agricultural burden and reduce the financial upheaval caused by the sabbatical and jubilee years.
166. *Talmud Bavli Hullin* 6b–7a.
167. *Talmud Bavli Hullin* 6b–7a.
168. *Talmud Yerushalmi Demai* 1.3 [22a] and *Talmud Yerushalmi Ta'anit* 3.1 [66b–c].
169. *Talmud Bavli Gittin* 60b.
170. This is based on an ambiguous verse, Psalm 119:126, which in context

could mean either "It is time *for us to act* for the Lord, because they [enemies] have broken your laws" or "It is time *for the Lord to act,* because they [enemies] have broken your laws." In Mishnah Berachot 9.5 and Talmud Bavli Berachot 63a the verse is taken out of context and interpreted in a third sense: "When it is time to act for the Lord, they [the rabbis] break your laws." In Talmud Bavli Gittin 60a this third reading is applied to writing down Oral Law lest it be forgotten. The Rabbis have broken the law by writing down the Oral Law, but in doing so they have acted for the Lord.

171. On page 47 of this volume, Heschel characterizes the work of Rabbi Judah Hanasi's grandfather, Rabbi Gamliel II, as an attempt to exorcise "particularism"—one-sided, uncompromising positions that fragment the community. Generations later, Rabbi Judah Hanasi was finally able to achieve the unity his forefathers sought.

172. He did study, however, with Rabbi Judah Hanasi.

173. Although Heschel puts it in quotation marks, this does not appear to be a direct quotation from Rabbinic literature. In *Talmud Bavli Ketubot* 103b and in *Talmud Bavli Bava Metzia* 85b there is a story in which Rabbi Hiyya explains how he will prevent Torah from disappearing, whereas in *Talmud Bavli Sukkah* 20b, Rabbi Hiyya is said to have come from Babylonia and restored Torah when it indeed was forgotten in Israel. The wording here is similar to a statement about Yehoshua ben Gamala in *Talmud Bavli Bava Batra* 21a.

174. *Talmud Bavli Sukkah* 20a. Here is the broader context: "At first, when the Torah was forgotten in Israel, Ezra came up from Babylonia and established it. Once again it was forgotten, and Hillel the Babylonian came up and established it. Once again it was forgotten, and Rabbi Hiyya and his sons came up and established it."

175. *Talmud Bavli Ketubot* 103b and *Talmud Bavli Bava Metzia* 85b. Rabbi Hiyya says this by way of contrast with Rabbi Hanina, who claims that if the Torah were forgotten he would be able to restore it by logical deduction. Rabbi Hiyya, on the other hand, commits to doing the many kinds of mundane but important work required to ensure that Torah will not be forgotten in the first place.

176. *Talmud Bavli Ketubot* 103b and *Talmud Bavli Bava Metzia* 85b.

177. *Talmud Bavli Mo'ed Katan* 16a–b. In the talmudic story, Rabbi Hiyya is teaching his two nephews in the marketplace.

178. *Talmud Bavli Yevamot* 63a–b.

179. *Talmud Bavli Yevamot* 63a.

180. *Talmud Bavli Hullin* 86a.

181. A paraphrase of Isaiah 46:11. Rabbi Judah Hanasi applies this verse to Rabbi Hiyya in *Talmud Bavli Menahot* 88b.

182. *Talmud Bavli Ketubot* 103b and *Talmud Bavli Bava Metzia* 85b. This is Rabbi Judah Hanasi's response to the passage about Rabbi Hiyya's method for preventing the loss of Torah.

183. *Talmud Bavli Kiddushin* 33a.

184. *Talmud Bavli Shabbat* 151b, paraphrased. Rabbi Hiyya's wife hears his remark as a prediction that his children will someday want for bread, and thus as a curse.

185. The fast was intended to bring rain to end a drought.

186. *Talmud Bavli Bava Metzia* 85b. In the Talmud, the story is somewhat different from the version Heschel quotes here. Elijah, and not Rabbi Hiyya, is punished with lashes. When the heavenly beings interrupt Rabbi Hiyya's prayer, asking, "Who has revealed the secret to the world," the answer is "Elijah." The talmudic story continues: "So they brought Elijah and gave him sixty flaming lashes. He went and disguised himself as a fiery bear, went among them [the people in the House of Learning], and scattered them."

187. *Talmud Bavli Hullin* 86a, paraphrased.

3. Don Yitzhak Abravanel

1. History has preserved little information about Abravanel's wife. Graetz describes her as "gracious and cultured" (Graetz, 4:340), but does not mention her name. Netanyahu reveals that Abravanel was "also the father of one and possibly two daughters," who seem to have stayed behind in Spain when the family fled (Netanyahu, 16; 269n36), and who are rarely mentioned.

2. King Afonso V of Portugal (1432–81). It was because of his ambitions to control the Moroccan coast of the Mediterranean that he was called "the African."

3. King Duarte was Afonso V's father.

4. *Halachah* refers to the legal material in Jewish literature; *aggadah* is legend and lore. Together, these terms are used to represent the entirety of traditional Jewish knowledge.

5. Abravanel, *Mif'alot Elohim* [The works of God], 8.6; *Commentary on the Former Prophets*, Joshua 1:6.

6. Yavetz, *Or hahayyim* [The light of life], 70. Maimonides's personal name was Moses. A popular phrase, etched on the headstone at his purported grave in Tiberias, likens Moses Maimonides (Rabbi Moses) to the biblical Moses (Moses our teacher): "From Moses to Moses, none

186

has arisen like Moses." Abravanel's remark is meant to distance himself from such exaggerated praise.

7. Abravanel, introduction to *Commentary on the Former Prophets*.

8. Leone Ebreo, Praise song for his father's *Commentary on the Latter Prophets*, included with the front matter of the printed edition.

9. Abravanel, introduction to *Commentary on the Former Prophets*.

10. The law imposed humiliating and damaging restrictions on Jews, including the requirement to wear a six-pointed red star on their clothing, the prohibition against traveling by mule, and the limitation of their right to own property outside designated Jewish areas.

11. Abravanel, introduction to *Commentary on the Former Prophets*.

12. Abravanel, introduction to *Commentary on the Former Prophets*. Here Abravanel quotes phrases from Psalm 140, vv. 4 and 5.

13. Abravanel, introduction to *Commentary on the Former Prophets*.

14. Abravanel, introduction to *Commentary on the Former Prophets*.

15. Leone Ebreo, Praise song.

16. Abravanel, *She'elot lehehacham Sha'ul Hakohen* [Questions to the sage Sha'ul Hakohen], 11c.

17. Leone Ebreo, Praise song.

18. Abravanel, *Commentary on the Former Prophets*, introduction to Kings.

19. Abravanel, *Commentary on the Former Prophets*, introduction to Kings.

20. Heschel includes this quotation in a footnote: "On 22 May 1492 the kings order the collecting of taxes that the communities and individuals owe Yitzhak Abravanel, who, as a Jew, is being expelled from the country. He transfers the offices he holds to the king, in order to be relieved of his tax collection responsibilities." Yitzhak Baer, *Die Juden im christlichen Spanien*, 2nd ed. (Berlin: Akademie-Verlag, 1936), 2:409. Further explanation is found in *Encyclopedia Judaica*, 2nd ed. (Detroit: Macmillan, 2007), 1:27. "Abravanel relinquished his claim to certain sums of money which he had advanced to Ferdinand and Isabella against tax-farming revenues, which he had not yet managed to recover. In return he was allowed to take 1000 gold ducats and various gold and silver valuables out of the country with him (May 31, 1492)."

21. Iovianus Pontano (1426–1503) was an Italian poet and humanist philosopher.

22. Heschel condenses here the complicated history of the three-way struggle among Ferrante I and the rulers of Spain and France for control of the kingdom of Naples. After much back and forth, Naples

was finally conquered in 1503 by Spain, in whose hands it remained into the following century.

23. Abravanel, *Commentary on the Former Prophets*, introduction to Kings.

24. Leone Ebreo, *Dialoghi d'Amore*, ed. C. Gebhardt (Heidelberg: C. Winter, 1929), "Regesten," document 19.

25. The Council of Ten was a governing body of the Republic of Venice.

26. Leone Ebreo, Praise song.

27. Abravanel, *She'elot lehehacham Sha'ul ha-Kohen*.

28. Leone Ebreo, Praise song.

29. Abravanel, introduction to *Rosh Amanah* [Principle of faith].

30. Judah Halevi (1075–1141) was a Spanish Jewish philosopher and poet. Like Abravanel, he valued the received traditions of Judaism over the truth claims of speculative philosophy.

31. Abravanel, *Ateret Zekenim* [Crown of the elders], chap. 12.

32. Abravanel, *Ateret Zekenim*, chap. 12.

33. Abravanel, *Mif'alot Elohim*, 1.1–2.

34. Maimonides, *Moreh Nevuchim* [Guide of the perplexed], 2.19.

35. Abravanel, *Mif'alot Elohim*, 1.3.

36. Maimonides, *Moreh Nevuchim*, 2.25.

37. Rabbi Nissim ben Reuven of Gerona (the "Ran") was a talmudic scholar who lived in Catalonia in the second half of the fourteenth century.

38. Crescas, *Or Hashem* [The light of the Lord], introduction to 3; 3.1.5.

39. Abravanel, *Mif'alot Elohim*, 1.3; see *Commentary on Maimonides's Moreh Nevuchim*, 2.19.

40. Gersonides, *Milhamot Hashem* [The wars of the Lord], 6.1.

41. Yehuda Halevi, *Kuzari*, 1.57.

42. Abravanel, *Mif'alot Elohim*, 2.1–5.

43. Abravanel, *Mif'alot Elohim*, 4.1, see Maimonides, *Moreh Nevuchim*, 3.15.

44. Abravanel, *Mif'alot Elohim*, 4.3–5; 5; and 6.

45. But see also Abravanel, *Mif'alot Elohim*, 9.9.

46. Abravanel, *Mif'alot Elohim*, 6.3.

47. Abravanel, *Mif'alot Elohim*, 1.

48. Abravanel, *Mif'alot Elohim*, 2. Heschel notes: "This thought also explains the possibility of miracles."

49. Abravanel, *Mif'alot Elohim*, 7.3. Heschel notes: "With Saadia he shares the claim of the possibility of the destruction of the world—also represented in Empedocles and Plato, and for which Abravanel can also bring evidence from aggadic writings."

50. Abravanel, *Mif'alot Elohim*, 7.4.

51. Abravanel, *Mif'alot Elohim*, 7.4.

52. Maimonides, *Moreh Nevuchim*, 3.13.
53. Nicholas of Cusa was a German Christian theologian and philosopher of Renaissance humanism.
54. Leone Ebreo, *Dialoghi d'Amore*, 3.76b.
55. Leone Ebreo, *Dialoghi d'Amore*, 3.144a–b.
56. Leone Ebreo, *Dialoghi d'Amore*, 3.144b–145a.
57. Leone Ebreo, *Dialoghi d'Amore*, 3.50a.
58. Leone Ebreo, *Dialoghi d'Amore*, 3.140b.
59. See Abravanel, *Mayanei Hayeshua* [Wellsprings of salvation], 12.6.
60. The son of Jesse refers to the Messiah. See Abravanel, introduction to *Yeshu'ot Meshiho* [Salvations of his anointed one].
61. Crescas, *Or Hashem*, 3.8.3; Albo, *Ikkarim*, 1.23, 4.42.
62. Heschel names these exegetes in a note: "Jehuda ben Bileam, Moses Gikatila, Chaim Galipapa, et al."
63. Messianic hope is the subject of the three works *Mayanei Hayeshua*, *Yeshu'ot Meshiho*, and *Mashmiya Yeshua* [Announcing salvation].
64. Abravanel, *Mayanei Hayeshua*, 12.7.
65. See Abravanel, *Mashmiya Yeshua*, 3.15; *Commentary on the Latter Prophets*, introduction to Isaiah.
66. Abravanel, *Commentary on the Torah*, Genesis 1.2.
67. Abravanel, *Commentary on the Latter Prophets*, Ezekiel 36:26.
68. Abravanel, *Mashmiya Yeshua*, 1.11.
69. Abravanel, *Commentary on the Latter Prophets,* introduction to Joel.
70. Chilianism, in the most literal sense, is the doctrine that Jesus will reign on earth for a thousand years, and then the world will end. Heschel is using the term to refer to any literalist, and potentially dangerous, form of messianism.
71. Asher Lämmlin was a Jew whose messianic claims whipped up fervor among many Jews and some Christians in Italy and Germany. His adherents fasted and prayed vehemently for a full year, in the expectation of immediate redemption. Their hopes were disappointed when Lämmlin abruptly disappeared, or perhaps died, with no sign of the Messiah on the horizon.
72. See his interpretations in *Yeshu'ot Meshiho*.
73. Rashi (Rabbi Shlomo ben Yitzhak, 1040–1105) was a French Jewish commentator whose notes on the Bible and the Talmud are included in almost all traditional publications of those texts. Many of his biblical commentaries are based on selections from ancient midrash.
74. Abraham Ibn Ezra (1089–1164) was a Spanish Jewish commentator whose particular interest was clarifying the language of the Bible.

75. Abravanel, introduction to *Commentary on the Former Prophets*; see *Commentary on the Torah*, introduction to Deuteronomy.

76. Abravanel, *Commentary on the Former Prophets*, 1 Samuel 4:4.

77. In the face of the 1492 edict requiring Jews to either convert to Christianity or leave Spain, it is estimated that between one hundred and two hundred thousand chose exile, while about half as many chose conversion.

78. Abravanel, *Commentary on the Latter Prophets*, introduction to Ezekiel.

79. Heschel notes: "Abravanel's critical stance toward Islamic philosophy, some features of his supernaturalism, as well as the formalism of his exegetical method show the influence of Christian scholasticism. Like several other works by Abravanel, his Hebrew translation of Thomas Aquinas's *Qaestio de Spiritualibus Creaturis* has not been preserved."

80. Leone Ebreo, *Dialoghi d'Amore*, 2.64b.

81. Leone Ebreo, *Dialoghi d'Amore*, 3.1a.

82. Abravanel, *Mashmiya Yeshua*, 2.3. Heschel notes: "Abravanel wrote a chronicle that spanned from Adam to his own time."

4. For the Jewish Holidays in Berlin

1. Variant of *Genesis Rabbah* 1.4, *Talmud Bavli Nedarim* 39b, and *Talmud Bavli Pesahim* 54a (commenting on Psalm 90:2–3).

2. *Midrash Tehillim* 90.12 (commenting on Psalm 90:2–3).

3. *Yalkut Shimoni* (Hosea 532) (commenting on Hosea 14:2).

4. *Talmud Bavli Yoma* 86b (commenting on Hosea 14:3).

5. *Lamentations Rabbah* 3.15.

6. *Pesikta Rabbati,* supplement 1 *piska* 3: "Return, O Israel" (commenting on Hosea 14:2).

7. Ezekiel 33:12. [The published essay reads "the guilt of the righteous," but that is probably an editorial slip.]

8. *Talmud Bavli Kiddushin* 40b (commenting on Ezekiel 33:12).

9. *Talmud Bavli Shabbat* 153a.

10. *Talmud Bavli Berachot* 12b (commenting on Ezekiel 16:63).

11. *Talmud Bavli Yoma* 86b.

12. As implied by Numbers 6:26.

13. As implied by Deuteronomy 10:17.

14. Variant of *Talmud Bavli Rosh Hashanah* 17b–18a.

15. *Levitucus Rabbah* 10.5.

16. *Talmud Bavli Yoma* 86a (commenting on Hosea 14:2).

17. Variant of *Leviticus Rabbah* 10.5. It is clear from the examples in the

original text that the decrees which stand to be cancelled are decrees of the heavenly court, not any human court.

18. *Talmud Bavli Yoma* 86b (commenting on Ezekiel 33:19).

19. *Talmud Bavli Yoma* 86a (commenting on Hosea 14:5).

20. *Talmud Bavli Yoma* 86b (commenting on Isaiah 59:20).

21. This passage is a midrashic reading of Isaiah 21:11–12.

22. *Talmud Yerushalmi Ta'anit* 1.1 [64a].

23. *Talmud Bavli Sanhedrin* 97b.

24. *Talmud Bavli Sanhedrin* 97b.

25. *Talmud Bavli Sanhedrin* 97b.

26. S. Buber, *Sifre de-Aggadeta al Megillat Esther, Midrash Panim Aheirim*, *nusah* 2, chap. 6 (1886).

27. *Pesikta Rabbati, piska* 44, "Return O Israel."

28. *Talmud Yerushalmi Ta'anit* 1.1 [64a] (commenting on Psalm 95:7).

29. *Talmud Bavli Yoma* 86b (commenting on Hosea 14:5).

30. This term refers to the writing on the wall in Daniel 5. In his arrogance, the king of Babylonia has thrown a feast in which he uses vessels stolen from the Temple for mundane and idolatrous purposes. A mysterious hand writes a message on the wall that is indecipherable until Daniel explains it: "*Mene*: God has numbered the days of your kingdom, and brought it to an end. *Tekel*: You have been weighed in the balance and found wanting." *Menetekel* has entered the German language as a word meaning "apocalyptic warning."

SELECTED BIBLIOGRAPHY

Archives and Manuscript Materials

AJHP. Abraham Joshua Heschel Papers. David M. Rubenstein Rare Book & Manuscript Library, Duke University Libraries, Durham NC.

"Das Gebet." Susannah Heschel Personal Archive, Newton MA.

"Das Leiden." Susannah Heschel Personal Archive, Newton MA.

Martin Buber Archive. National Library of Israel, Jerusalem.

Published Works

Abravanel, Yitzhak. *Ateret Zekenim.* Amsterdam: Orphans of Solomon Proops, 1730. http://www.hebrewbooks.org/23712.

———. *Commentary on the Former Prophets.* Jerusalem: Torah v'Daas, 1960. http://www.hebrewbooks.org/14367.

———. *Commentary on the Latter Prophets.* Jerusalem: Torah v'Daas, 1960. http://www.hebrewbooks.org/14369.

———. *Commentary on the Torah.* Venice: Bragadini, 1579. http://www.hebrewbooks.org/44335.

———. *Mashmiya Yeshua.* Offenbach: Hirsch Segal Spitz, 1767. http://www.hebrewbooks.org/19481.

———. *Mayanei Hayeshua.* Stettin: R. Grossmann und E. Schrenzel, 1860. http://www.hebrewbooks.org/33861.

———. *Mif'alot Elohim.* Venice: John de Gara, 1592. http://hebrewbooks.org/11780.

———. *Rosh Amanah.* Venice: Marc Antonio Giustiniani, 1545. http://www.hebrewbooks.org/11860.

———. *She'elot lehe-hacham Sha'ul Hakohen.* Venice: John de Gara, 1574. http://www.hebrewbooks.org/11866.

———. *Yeshu'ot Meshicho.* Karlsruhe: 1828. http://www.hebrewbooks.org/19605.

193

Avot de Rabbi Natan A and *B*. Ramat Gan: Bar Ilan University, 2012. The Responsa Project CD, version 20.

Brenner, Michael. *The Renaissance of Jewish Culture in Weimar Germany*. New Haven: Yale University Press, 1996.

Cohen, Shaye. *From the Maccabees to the Mishnah*. 3rd ed. Louisville KY: Westminster John Knox Press, 2014.

Crescas, Hasdai. *Or Hashem*. Jerusalem: Sifre Ramot, 1990. http://www .hebrewbooks.org/22063.

Ecclesiastes Rabbah. Ramat Gan: Bar Ilan University, 2012. The Responsa Project CD, version 20.

Fonrobert, Charlotte Elisheva and Martin S. Jaffee. *The Cambridge Companion to the Talmud and Rabbinic Literature*. Cambridge: Cambridge University Press, 2007.

Freeden, Herbert. *The Jewish Press in the Third Reich*. Providence RI: Berg, 1993.

Genesis Rabbah. Ramat Gan: Bar Ilan University, 2012. The Responsa Project CD, version 20.

Gersonides, *Milhamot Hashem*. Berlin: Louis Lamm, 1923. http://www .hebrewbooks.org/53594.

Graetz, Heinrich. *History of the Jews*. Vol. 2, *From the Reign of Hyrcanus (135 BCE) to the Completion of the Babylonian Talmud (500 CE)*, translated by Philipp Bloch. Philadelphia: Jewish Publication Society of America, 1902.

———. *History of the Jews*. Vol. 4, *From the Rise of the Kabbala (1270 CE) to the Permanent Settlement of the Marranos in Holland (1618 CE)*, translated by Philipp Bloch. Philadelphia: Jewish Publication Society of America, 1956.

Hebrew Bible. Ramat Gan: Bar Ilan University, 2012. The Responsa Project CD, version 20.

Heschel, Abraham Joshua. *Don Yitzhak Abravanel*. Berlin: Erich Reiss Verlag, 1937.

———. "Das Gebet," *Bulletin of Congregation Habonim at Central Synagogue*, no. 11 (September 1941): 2–3.

———. "Die Kraft der Buße, 1936." *Gemeindeblatt der jüdischen Gemeinde zu Berlin* 26, no. 37 (September 13, 1936): 4.

———. "Die Marranen von Heute." *Gemeindeblatt der jüdischen Gemeinde zu Berlin* 26, no. 38 (September 16, 1936): 2.

———. "Elischa ben Abuja." *Gemeindeblatt der jüdischen Gemeinde zu Berlin* 26, no. 17 (April 26, 1936): 16.

———. "Jewish Education." In *The Insecurity of Freedom*, 223–41. New York: Schocken, 1972.

————. "Lichter über dem Meer." *Gemeindeblatt der jüdischen Gemeinde zu Berlin* 27, no. 48 (November 29, 1937): 4.

————. *Maimonides, A Biography*. Translated by Joachim Neugroschel. New York: Farrar, Straus and Giroux, 1982.

————. *Man's Quest for God*. Santa Fe NM: Aurora Press, 1998.

————. "The Meaning of Repentance." In *Moral Grandeur and Spiritual Audacity: Essays by Abraham Joshua Heschel*. Edited by Susannah Heschel. New York: Farrar, Straus and Giroux, 1997.

————. "Rabbi Akiba." *Gemeindeblatt der jüdischen Gemeinde zu Berlin* 26, no. 13 (March 29, 1936): 16.

————. "Rabbi Chiya." *Gemeindeblatt der jüdischen Gemeinde zu Berlin* 26, no. 33 (August 6, 1936): 15.

————. "Rabbi Gamliel II." *Gemeindeblatt der jüdischen Gemeinde zu Berlin* 26, no. 15 (March 8, 1936): 15.

————. "Rabbi Jehuda Ha-Nassi." *Gemeindeblatt der jüdischen Gemeinde zu Berlin* 26, no. 33 (May 31, 1936): 15.

————. "Rabbi Jochanan ben Zakkai." *Gemeindeblatt der jüdischen Gemeinde zu Berlin* 26, no. 8 (February 23, 1936): 14.

————. "Rabbi Meir." *Gemeindeblatt der jüdischen Gemeinde zu Berlin* 26, no. 20 (May 17, 1936): 16.

————. "Rabbi Schimon ben Gamliel II." *Gemeindeblatt der jüdischen Gemeinde zu Berlin*, 16, no. 15 (April 12, 1936): 15.

————. "Rückkehr." *Mitteilungsblatt der Theodor Herzl Society* 14 (December 29, 1939): 1–2.

————. "The Spirit of Jewish Education." *Jewish Education* 24, no. 2 (Fall 1953): 9–19, 62.

————. "Witness to Sefardic Jewry's Descent to Agony: First International Translation of 'Don Jizchak Abravanel.'" Translated by William Wolf. *Intermountain Jewish News*, Chanukah Edition, Literary Supplement (December 19, 1986): 5–6, 8–12.

Jaffee, Martin S. *Early Judaism*. Upper Saddle River NJ: Prentice Hall, 1997.

Jay, Martin. "1920: The Free Jewish School Is Founded in Frankfurt am Main under the Leadership of Franz Rosenzweig." In *Yale Companion to Jewish Writing and Thought in German Culture, 1096–1996*, edited by Sander L. Gilman and Jack Zipes, 395–400. New Haven: Yale University Press, 1997.

Josephus, Flavius. *Complete Works*. Grand Rapids: Kregel, 1950.

Kaplan, Edward K. and Samuel H. Dresner. *Abraham Joshua Heschel: Prophetic Witness*. New Haven: Yale University Press, 1998.

Lamentations Rabbah. Ramat Gan: Bar Ilan University, 2012. The Responsa Project CD, version 20.

Lau, Binyamin. *The Sages: Character, Context and Creativity*. Vol.1, *The Second Temple Period*, translated by Michael Prawer. Jerusalem: Koren, 2010.

Lau, Binyamin. *The Sages: Character, Context and Creativity*. Vol. 2, *From Yavneh to the Bar Kokhba Revolt*, translated by Ilana Kurshan. Jerusalem: Koren, 2011.

Lau, Binyamin. *The Sages: Character, Context and Creativity*. Vol. 3, *The Galilean Period*, translated by Ilana Kurshan. Jerusalem: Koren, 2013.

Leviticus Rabbah. Ramat Gan: Bar Ilan University, 2012. The Responsa Project CD, version 20.

Marmur, Michael. "Traditional Exemplars in a Time of Crisis." In *Between Jewish Tradition and Modernity: Rethinking an Old Opposition*, edited by Michael A. Meyer and David N. Myers, 192–208. Detroit: Wayne State University Press, 2014.

Mechilta deRabbi Ishmael. Ramat Gan: Bar Ilan University, 2012. The Responsa Project CD, version 20.

Midrash Mishlei. Ramat Gan: Bar Ilan University, 2012. The Responsa Project CD, version 20.

Minor Tractates. Ramat Gan: Bar Ilan University, 2012. The Responsa Project CD, version 20.

Mishnah. Ramat Gan: Bar Ilan University, 2012. The Responsa Project CD, version 20.

Netanyahu, Benzion. *Don Isaac Abravanel, Statesman and Philosopher*. 5th ed., rev. and updated. Ithaca NY: Cornell University Press, 1998.

Numbers Rabbah. Ramat Gan: Bar Ilan University, 2012. The Responsa Project CD, version 20.

Pesikta Rabbati. Ramat Gan: Bar Ilan University, 2012. The Responsa Project CD, version 20.

Rosenzweig, Franz. *On Jewish Learning*. New York: Schocken Books, 1965.

Roth, Norman. *Medieval Jewish Civilization: An Encyclopedia*. New York: Routledge, 2003.

Ruth Rabbah. Ramat Gan: Bar Ilan University, 2012. The Responsa Project CD, version 20.

Schiffman, Lawrence H. *From Text to Tradition: A History of Second Temple and Rabbinic Judaism*. Hoboken NJ: Ktav, 1991.

Schwartz, Seth. *Imperialism and Jewish Society, 200 BCE to 640 CE*. Princeton: Princeton University Press, 2001.

Sifre Deuteronomy. Ramat Gan: Bar Ilan University, 2012. The Responsa Project CD, version 20.

Talmud Bavli. Ramat Gan: Bar Ilan University, 2012. The Responsa Project CD, version 20.

Talmud Yerushalmi. Ramat Gan: Bar Ilan University, 2012. The Responsa Project CD, version 20.

Tosefta. Ramat Gan: Bar Ilan University, 2012. The Responsa Project CD, version 20.

Trend, J. B. and H. Loewe, eds. *Isaac Abravanel: Six Lectures.* Cambridge: Cambridge University Press, 1937.

Urbach, Ephraim E. *The Sages: Their Concepts and Beliefs.* Translated by Israel Abrahams. Cambridge MA: Harvard University Press, 1975.

Yalkut Shimoni. Ramat Gan: Bar Ilan University, 2012. The Responsa Project CD, version 20.

Yavetz, Joseph. *Or ha-hayyim.* Przemysl: Mordecai Jonah Rosenfeld, 1873. http://www.hebrewbooks.org/38293.

CONTRIBUTORS

MARION FABER is professor of German emerita, Swarthmore College. She is author of *Angels of Daring: Tightrope Walker and Acrobat in Nietzsche, Kafka, Rilke and Thomas Mann* (1980); coauthor with Stephen Lehmann of *Rudolf Serkin: A Life* (2003); and translator of many books, including two she translated with Stephen Lehmann: *Human, All Too Human* by Friedrich Nietzsche (1984) and *The Tables of the Law* by Thomas Mann (2010).

SUSANNAH HESCHEL is the Eli Black Professor of Jewish Studies and chair of the program at Dartmouth College. Her numerous publications include *Abraham Geiger and the Jewish Jesus*, winner of a National Jewish Book Award, and *The Aryan Jesus: Christian Theologians and the Bible in Nazi Germany*. The daughter of Abraham Joshua Heschel, she has also edited several books, including *Moral Grandeur and Spiritual Audacity: Essays of Abraham Joshua Heschel* and *Betrayal: German Churches and the Holocaust* (with Robert P. Ericksen). She holds fellowships from the Ford Foundation and the Carnegie Foundation, and a Guggenheim Fellowship.

STEPHEN LEHMANN was Humanities Bibliographer at the University of Pennsylvania. He is coauthor with Marion Faber of *Rudolf Serkin: A Life* (2003) and translator of several books, including two with Marion Faber: *Human, All Too Human* by Friedrich Nietzsche (1984) and *The Tables of the Law* by Thomas Mann (2010).

HELEN PLOTKIN is the director of the Swarthmore College Center for the Study of Classical Jewish Texts. She teaches courses in Biblical Hebrew and in classical Hebrew texts at Swarthmore; directs Mekom Torah, a Philadelphia-area Jewish community learning project; writes for online journals including Tablet magazine; and lectures widely.